Integrity and Agreement

Economics Cognition and Society

This series provides a forum for theoretical and empirical investigations of social phenomena. It promotes works that focus on the interactions among cognitive processes, individual behavior, and social outcomes. It is especially open to interdisciplinary books that are genuinely integrative.

Titles in the Series

Glenn R. Parker. *Capitol Investments: The Marketability of Political Skills*
Lanse Minkler. *Integrity and Agreement: Economics When Principles also Matter*
Stephen T. Ziliak and Deirdre N. McCloskey. *The Cult of Statistical Significance: How the Standard Error Costs Us Jobs, Justice, and Lives*
Eirik G. Furubotn and Rudolf Richter. *Institutions and Economic Theory: The Contribution of the New Institutional Economics,* Second Edition
Tyler Cowen. *Markets and Cultural Voices: Liberty vs. Power in the Lives of Mexican Amate Painters*
Thráinn Eggertsson. *Imperfect Institutions: Possibilities and Limits of Reform*
Vernon W. Ruttan. *Social Science Knowledge and Economic Development: An Institutional Design Perspective*
Phillip J. Nelson and Kenneth V. Greene. *Signaling Goodness: Social Rules and Public Choice*
Stephen Knack, Editor. *Democracy, Governance, and Growth*
Omar Azfar and Charles A. Cadwell, Editors. *Market-Augmenting Government: The Institutional Foundations for Prosperity*
Randall G. Holcombe. *From Liberty to Democracy: The Transformation of American Government*
David T. Beito, Peter Gordon, and Alexander Tabarrok, Editors. *The Voluntary City: Choice, Community, and Civil Society*
Alexander J. Field. *Altruistically Inclined? The Behavioral Sciences, Evolutionary Theory, and the Origins of Reciprocity*
David George. *Preference Pollution: How Markets Create the Desires We Dislike*
Julian L. Simon. *The Great Breakthrough and Its Cause*
E. L. Jones. *Growth Recurring: Economic Change in World History*
Rosemary L. Hopcroft. *Regions, Institutions, and Agrarian Change in European History*
Lee J. Alston, Gary D. Libecap, and Bernardo Mueller. *Titles, Conflict, and Land Use: The Development of Property Rights and Land Reform on the Brazilian Amazon Frontier*

(continues on last page)

Integrity and Agreement

Economics When Principles Also Matter

Lanse Minkler

THE UNIVERSITY OF MICHIGAN PRESS • Ann Arbor

Published in the United States of America by
The University of Michigan Press
Manufactured in the United States of America
⊗ Printed on acid-free paper

2011 2010 2009 2008 4 3 2 1

A CIP catalog record for this book is available from the British Library.

Library of Congress Cataloging-in-Publication Data

Minkler, Lanse.
Integrity and agreement : economics when principles also matter / Lanse Minkler.
p. cm. — (Economics, cognition, and society)
Includes bibliographical references and index.
ISBN-13: 978-0-472-11643-0 (cloth : alk. paper)
ISBN-10: 0-472-11643-6 (cloth : alk. paper)
1. Economics—Moral and ethical aspects. 2. Integrity. 3. Self-interest. 4. Truthfulness and falsehood. 5. Choice (Psychology) I. Title. II. Title: Economics when principles also matter.
HB72.M52 2008
174—dc22 2007052489

For my parents and my brother.

And to all those who do as they say
without expecting a big parade.

Contents

Acknowledgments

My great teachers have included Kostas Scoulas, Jerry Sanders, Moshe Adler, Christopher Titmus, José Reissig, and Sharda Rogell. I'm grateful to each for teaching me to challenge my current views as a way of coming closer to truth.

In writing this book, I have benefited from the skilled readings and advice of many people. I'm grateful to Donald Baxter, James Boudreau, John Davis, Dhammika Dharmapala, Margaret Gilbert, Shareen Hertel, Vicki Knoblauch, John Rickards, Jonathan Wight, Richard Ashby Wilson, and a number of anonymous reviewers. Even when I did not include their comments, each undoubtedly improved the clarity of ideas in this volume.

I am indebted to Metin Cosgel and Thomas Miceli, my coauthors on previously published articles about integrity. I am grateful for their willingness to work on the topic, and their skillful contributions that enhanced this project. I also thank Metin and Tom for providing helpful comments on different chapters.

Timur Kuran, the series editor, did a remarkable job editing this book. He painstakingly read and provided detailed comments on a couple different drafts. The wise advice derived from his careful scrutiny clearly improved the quality of this book, sometimes in spite of my own resistances.

Finally, I am most grateful to my wife, Fé Delos-Santos. Not only did she eagerly participate in many lively debates about the ideas in this book, she also expertly edited many chapter drafts, as well as an early version of the whole thing. Because she is a lover of great literature and great writing, I want to publicly acknowledge her torment.

Chapter 1

Why Integrity?

Consider the proposition "lying is wrong." True or false? My experience has shown that most people quickly answer "true." Not surprisingly, the question tends to be a little more problematic for economists.

The first time I asked someone whether lying is wrong, it was of a job candidate. When she dutifully asked what I was working on I innocently asked the question above to help explain. The look on her face was a mixture of confusion and terror. I wasn't trying to trick her, but I could sense her apprehension in weighing her options. If she answered "true," she might have thought I would not think her a good economist, while if she answered "false," I might spring some fancy ethical trap. Had she answered "false" it likely would have been because she realized that economists don't deal much with ethics. We deal with preferences and rationality, and thus verbal claims against preferences are just noncredible "cheap talk." Her hesitancy signaled she was not a certain type of naturalist, for whom ethical questions like the one posed are nonsense, in which case she could have immediately blurted out "false." On the other hand, she may have had some faint recollection about the notions of right and wrong from before her graduate training and thought that somehow she should answer "true."[1] Her dilemma was apparent. She decided against either response, and after some awkward mumbling we talked instead about New England's strange weather.

Since the question refers to a moral principle, it asks about one's understanding of the world. Were one to thoroughly embrace the principle, so much so that it formed part of one's identity, we might be able to say that the person was a person of integrity. In that case, to violate a moral principle the person takes to be true (by lying) would be to act contrary to her own under-

1. She might also have objected to the categorical nature of the question. Many I have asked wanted to say "true," but could think of exceptions like lying to prevent harm or "white lies." I will discuss those qualifications in detail later, but when I modify the proposition to "lying is wrong in normal circumstances," it really doesn't seem to change the number of "true" and "false" answers.

standing of the world and thus her understanding of her own self as well, which would be incoherent. Even in a weaker case, one more consistent with current economic theory, if the person did not identify with the moral principle but instead had a strong preference over it, she would still have reason not to lie.

In this book I will develop the notion of two different kinds of integrity. One focuses on identity-conferring commitments to principles, the other on preferences for principles. But while they differ in their particulars, most fundamentally, both refer to honest behavior. The possibility of integrity and honest behavior is important any time there are economic agreements.[2] That covers a lot of economics. This book will cover informal interactions that characterize social dilemmas, formal legal agreements between buyers and sellers, political agreements, employment agreements, religious agreements, and the social contract. In each of these cases, the possibility of integrity changes the answers given by neoclassical economics and instrumental rationality (rational decision making in one's own self-interest) because *to make an agreement that one has no intention of honoring is to lie.* This simple but powerful fact seems to have eluded most economic analyses.

The analysis here will not require heroic assumptions. We will not focus on the few individuals who might embrace myriad moral principles and possess the kind of strength of will that, like Don Quixote, leads them to try to right every wrong. But neither will we confine ourselves to the kind of lead character presented in Ben Jonson's play *Volpone.* While nothing prevents a rational economic man from *also* being moral, when it comes to economic agreements, he is most often characterized as opportunistic.[3] More beautifully articulated, Volpone is ruthlessly selfish and engages in

> . . . sanctimonious speeches, lust and possessiveness poorly disguised as love and marriage, cynical legalism passing itself off as pure justice, boastful name-dropping that pretends cultural sophistication, snobbery congratulating itself that it is decorum, and greed deluding itself that it is really prudence, responsibility, even religion.[4]

2. Earlier works that touch on the importance of honesty in economic interactions include Sen 1978, Adler 1992, and Bowles 1998.

3. One might protest that self-interest is fundamentally moral in and of itself. Indeed, Holmes (1990) persuasively argues that self-interest as developed by Adam Smith and his contemporaries did provide a contrast to the prevailing doctrines of honor and original sin, and that universal self-interest is egalitarian and democratic because it requires respect for everyone's interests. Nevertheless, moral philosophers usually maintain that when it comes to the moral behavior of an individual, the moral rightness of any act is independent of what the person might prefer.

4. Jonson 2003, ix.

Even though Volpone provides a colorful foil for the ruthlessly moral Don Quixote, we will instead focus most of our attention on a normal person in normal economic circumstances. Like most of us, she takes at least some principles seriously, but she also has to grapple with other considerations, most notably her own preferences and tempting rationalizations. But we do know that average people in real life do keep their agreements *even when they could cheat.* Plumbers sometimes do as they say, workers do provide good efforts, business partners don't cheat each other, contractors keep their agreements, people follow their religious vows, and even politicians sometimes do what they promise. These kinds of honored agreements are what make the economy and society work.

It will be necessary to aim a fair amount of attention at the existence of principles. Sometimes principles are taken to be truths or laws or as starting points for reasoning. As I have already suggested, I characterize principles as general propositions that can be taken as either true or false. Once a principle is accepted as true, it provides a sort of universality that applies to beliefs and actions. If I accept "lying is wrong" as true, I am not free to interpret it as meaning I have to tell the truth only to right-handed people but not necessarily to left-handed people. There may be exceptional cases like lying to prevent great harm, but most candidates for such exceptions fail a meaningful-relevance test. Moreover, this universal character also applies no matter what my preferences are. I may not *want* to tell the truth to some left-handed person, but that doesn't mean that "lying is wrong" suddenly becomes false. The principle holds in spite of my own preferences. Thus principles and preferences are different, and so both will be included in the analyses in this book.

While preferences and principles are independent from one another, individuals still possess preferences over principles. I possess a preference over "lying is wrong" to the extent that if I act on that principle I may receive positive utility. The more important point now is that it is the existence of principles that forms the basis for one kind of integrity, *commitment-integrity,* and the preference for principles that forms another kind, *preference-integrity.* The former requires individuals to make judgments about the truth or falsity of principles, while the latter only requires a complete preference mapping.

If individuals recognize the existence of principles and include them in their decision-making process, the next question becomes which one or ones should we focus on. While some of the analysis will consider additional principles, the principle I have already referred to, "lying is wrong," turns out to be both fundamental and also the principle most relevant for economic agreements. Virtually all religious and philosophical traditions counsel against lying, even if they differ in their justifications and exceptions.[5] It holds the same elevated status as "murdering innocents is wrong" in most traditions, in the sense of its barely qualified condemnation. The principle is also most relevant for economic agreements because all agreements are representations, and lying is an intentional misrepresentation. Therefore, most of the analysis centers on what I call the *minimalist principle,* "lying is wrong." And by basing it on just one fundamental principle, the analysis stays more tractable.

To what extent do people base their acts on principled decision making? As an empirical matter we do know that the behavioral postulate of instrumental rationality is violated with great regularity. Most commentators on the subject have pointed to commonplace behaviors not involving agreements, like tipping, tax paying, voting, contributing to public goods, and helping others when there is no chance of reciprocity. Sometimes people are even heroic.[6] Overwhelming experimental evidence also shows that people often cooperate against their material interests. Experimenters use social dilemmas like a Prisoner's Dilemma or voluntary contribution to a public good where, based on instrumental rationality, the dominant strategy is to defect. But consistently great numbers do not defect, even where there is anonymity and the game is played only once.[7] In his meta-analysis of 37 different studies consisting of 130 distinct social dilemma experiments, David Sally calculates a mean cooperation rate of 47.4 percent for the entire pooled sample.[8] The 2002 award of the Nobel Prize in Economics to psychologist Daniel Kahneman decisively legitimated the behavioralist school with its critique of instrumental rationality.[9] That does not mean, however, that instrumental rationality is not still a useful theoretical construct or a good first empirical approximation. The findings of the behavioralist school (and perhaps others) may yet be incorporated. One of the virtues of neoclassical economics is that it can fold new ideas and findings into its considerable maw, sometimes almost seamlessly (witness models of imperfect information).

It also seems beyond question that many normal people in normal circumstances have an aversion to lying for material gain. Again, the limited ex-

5. See Bok 1978, which I will often refer to and will discuss in some detail in chapter 5.

6. Evidence and analysis of rescuing and heroic behavior is discussed in Mansbridge 1998.

7. See, for instance, Marwell and Ames 1981; Schneider and Pommerehne 1981; Caporael, Dawes, Orbell, and van de Kragt 1989; Davis and Holt 1993; Frey and Bohnet 1995; and Ledyard 1995.

8. Sally 1995, 62. Also see Ledyard's (1995) review for similar findings. Caporael, Dawes, Orbell, and van de Kragt (1989) provide particularly good evidence against self-interested behavior as normally conceived.

9. See Kahneman 2003 for a brief review of the evidence against "selfishness," rationality, and unchanging tastes.

isting evidence is supportive. One empirical regularity in experimental settings is that communication significantly increases cooperation.[10] More to the point, David Sally estimates in his meta-analysis that (noncredible) promises to cooperate elicited by experimenters increase cooperation by 12 to 30 percent, depending on the regression model.[11] That finding in particular suggests that even people in contrived situations recognize and act on the minimalist principle. More recently, Uri Gneezy experimentally tested the propensity to lie by varying the harm that lying causes. His main finding is that "the average person prefers not to lie, when doing so only increases her payoff a little but reduces the other's payoff a great deal."[12] Social psychologists similarly find that most lies are "white lies" aimed at affecting the perceptions of others rather than lies with the purpose of material gain.[13]

Finally, for admittedly unconventional evidence, consider the offerings of classical literature. I have already mentioned Don Quixote, Cervantes's beloved but doomed character who unrelentingly champions good. Don Quixote embraces all moral principles, delusionally perhaps, and repeatedly puts his and his squire's life on the line to defend them. Or consider Joseph Conrad's *Lord Jim*. Jim is the confident, flawlessly principled sea ship officer. Yet in one inexplicable moment, he abandons his ship loaded with passengers when he believes it to be hopelessly doomed. Jim then spends the rest of his life trying to recover the sense of himself that he himself deserted. In one case we affectionately root for the character who fights for the impossible, in the other we sympathetically mourn for the one who abandons that which seems so possible. The kinds of affection and sympathy that these characters have evoked in generations of readers is deeply felt because integrity matters. Don Quixote represents the flawed man who reaches for perfection—unattainable integrity; and Jim, the ideal man who falls from grace—lost integrity. We are

---

10. John Ledyard in his 1995 chapter on public goods in the *Handbook of Experimental Economics* concludes that the evidence on pre-play communication counts as a "strong effect" that increases cooperation. For instance, Dawes, McTavish, and Shaklee (1977) report that payoffs increased from 31 to 71 percent when relevant communication was allowed in one-shot games. Isaac and Walker (1988) find contribution rates of over 80 percent in one-shot public goods type games with communication, and over 90 percent in repeated games.

11. Sally 1995, 78.

12. Gneezy 2005, 385.

13. DePaulo et al. (1996) examined the daily diaries of 77 college students and 70 communities to come to this conclusion. While they do find evidence that some lies are told for personal advantage, they "think that lies are less often told in the pursuit of goals such as financial gain and material advantage and instead are much more often told in the pursuit of psychic rewards such as esteem, affection, and respect" (981). Such lies are also told to minimize the tension with, and hurt feelings of, others. Thus, these kinds of lies are not seen as serious by the liars.

moved by their stories time and again because we think integrity is real and important.

Still, I cannot claim that the evidence suggests that principled behavior or integrity is ubiquitous. People are certainly interested in integrity—in 2005 it was the most looked-up word on Merriam-Webster's Web site.[14] And it may turn out that integrity is more pervasive than we know, we just haven't really looked carefully enough. To the extent that it is desirable, we might look into ways of increasing its frequency (the topic of chapter 9). Of course, adding integrity to the motivational mix might only add to the cost of complexity with little or insufficient benefit. That could be the methodological position of those embracing Milton Friedman's positivism, or some version of it.[15] On that view, a good theory is one that predicts well, quite apart from the realism of the theory's assumptions. When combined with Occam's razor, the best theory becomes the one with the simplest assumptions that also predicts best. I would call this view *methodological simplicity,* and, especially when considering the already staggering complexity of some economic models, simplicity is a virtue.

But I think *methodological realism* is better. In the version that I favor, we should aim for a theory whose assumptions and predictions are *both* true. That is, both the theory's assumptions *and* predictions should aim to correspond to the way things really are, or possibly could be. On this view, the real world exists independently of what we think about it. Our histories, values, and biases may affect the selection of our theoretical analyses, but the intention is to bring our thinking into correspondence with the objective, existing state of affairs, at least to the extent that we can.[16] Of course the goal of some theorizing may be simply to develop models that are logically and internally consistent without reference to the world. The goal of those kinds of analysis too is a kind of logical truth. But if the pursuit of truth contains some reference to the real world, it seems incongruent to insist on truth in one aspect of

14. Associated Press report, *Hartford Courant,* December 11, 2005.

15. Friedman 1953.

16. One can find many different brands of realism in the literature on methodology (e.g., Maki 1988; Lawson 1997). There are a lot of interesting epistemological and ontological issues. My view is that there is an objectively existing real world, we can possibly know that world, the aim of economic theory is to accurately represent that world, and a theory is better than another if it *more* accurately represents the world. Because such representations are subject to human comprehension, to say that one theory more accurately represents the world leaves open the possibility of interpretation and thus persuasion. Moreover, our thinking can also *change* the world because thinking precedes acts and acts change the world. One kind of thinking has changed the world by introducing genocidal acts; another has changed it by reducing or eliminating disease. But to the extent that we truly understand the world, we may be able to intentionally affect it with corresponding policies.

a theory (e.g., implications) but not another (e.g., assumptions). If we are committed to seeking the truth about the world, we should not partition it selectively.

The concern about the added complexity of real assumptions is legitimate, however. The assumptions that we do make should be true, but that does not answer the question about how many true assumptions we should include in our analyses. The issue becomes one of balancing the costs and benefits, and reasonable people may disagree. In this book, beyond instrumental rationality—an assumption I think is true for many people at many different times—I will only add one further assumption in the case of preference-integrity, namely, that a preference for honesty exists, and one set of assumptions in the case of commitment-integrity, namely, those relating to moral principles. This added realism generates novel implications.

As a preview, here are a few of the more interesting implications generated by incorporating one version or another of integrity into analyses of economic agreements. By including the possibility of preference-integrity in Prisoner's Dilemma–type interactions, modeled as a continuum of types, we will see that three distinct types of players emerge. Perhaps most important, a sufficient amount of integrity results in higher payoffs by promoting a critical amount of cooperation. Trust results from honesty, not vice versa. With respect to legal contracts, integrity can be consistent with contractual breach, but not fraud. In the political arena, either kind of integrity reduces political shirking (voting against constituents' interests) and can help explain why legislators don't change their votes in their last term of office. In the employment context, adding commitment-integrity leads to an implication that contrasts starkly with the literature on the theory of the firm. Whereas the received literature focuses on employee (or contractor) shirking and then recommends monitoring, incentive contracts, and hierarchy, the analysis presented here implies that creating clear, fair agreements will take care of misaligned expectations, which leaves the door open for focusing on the coordination of different input contributions, especially knowledge ones—the real essence of the firm. We will also see that adding integrity can help to solve some of the anomalies in the economics-of-religion literature. For instance, a person of religious integrity has reason to engage in counterpreferential behaviors like refraining from eating forbidden foods, even in private. As a last example, we will see that, based on the minimalist principle, a person of commitment-integrity also has reason to support a more general social contract like human rights, under some fairly routine conditions.

Two concepts in particular drive the analysis: *mutual deceit* and *coherence.* Mutual deceit pertains to the minimalist principle "lying is wrong." Not surprisingly, there are some contexts in which it is morally acceptable to lie, like buying and selling at a bazaar. Economic agents themselves will treat some, but not all, situations as ones of mutual deceit. When contractual partners do not consent to lies, however, integrity does indeed matter. So a lot of emphasis will be placed on the context of economic agreements. Coherence, on the other hand, is a normative requirement of commitment-integrity. To illustrate, if one commits to the minimalist principle but then lies wildly, that is a form of incoherence. Lying to a left-handed but not to a right-handed person is also incoherent. Normatively, in either case, such a person could not be said to be a person of integrity. As a positive matter, some people surely recognize this coherence requirement and behave accordingly. Others may fail to act coherently because of a weak will, self-deception, errors in judgment, or moral exclusion—all factors that will further contribute to the analysis.

To my knowledge, no other book has used integrity as the basis to study agreements. Nevertheless, several pioneering studies have touched on the same, or closely related, issues. Perhaps most central has been Amartya Sen's illuminating use of commitments as something different from preferences.[17] While philosophers have recognized the distinction for centuries, it has been a significant departure for economists only recently.

Other major works often focus on altruism or cooperation. For instance, Robert Frank, in his seminal book *Passions Within Reason* (1988), asks how mutually beneficial interactions could occur in a world populated by both selfish and cooperative people. By using evolutionary processes as a metaphor, people are predisposed to either cooperate or act selfishly. If cooperators can interact with each other they get a higher joint payoff than when selfish people interact with each other. But, as in a Prisoner's Dilemma game, the highest payoff goes to those selfish people who can interact with cooperators. The problem is, how can cooperators credibly commit to actually behaving cooperatively? Frank's answer is that cooperation is a moral trait subject to evolutionary forces (i.e., it must confer an important advantage), and that emotions both sustain and signal the presence of this moral trait. If detecting this signal in others requires a resource cost, Frank finds an evolutionarily stable equilibrium such that cooperators and selfish people exist simultaneously. Justifiably, Frank's approach and model have been enormously influential.

The real difference lies in our different approaches. While Frank locates moral behavior in the emotions, and also gives them a strategic role, my analysis locates moral behavior in the existence of a preference for honesty in the case of preference-integrity, and conscious and reflective deliberation in the case of commitment-integrity. While Frank's analysis follows philosopher

17. Sen 1978.

David Hume because moral behavior stems from irrational moral sentiments, mine features the usual notion of rationality in the case of preference-integrity and, in the case of commitment-integrity, follows philosopher Immanuel Kant because moral behavior stems more from a person's ability to reason. That is not to say our accounts are incompatible; it is to say they are conceptually quite distinct (more on this in chapter 4).

Commitment-integrity, in particular, is also conceptually quite different from those preference-based accounts that similarly emphasize cooperative, social, and/or moral behavior. For instance, in *Not Just for the Money,* Bruno Frey (1997a) builds the case that people sometimes engage in behaviors simply because they like to. People might do a good job at work because they like to; they may vote because they like civic participation; they may give blood or help another because they want to indulge their altruistic preferences. Borrowing from the psychology literature, the key insight is that sometimes people will indulge these kinds of preferences *less* often when there are incentives to act on them. Sometimes such extrinsic interventions can crowd out intrinsic motivations, particularly if the interventions are seen as controlling. So, sometimes people just enjoy doing a good job, and incentives to work hard may actually reduce such efforts. I will consider the issue more fully in chapter 6, but doing a good job because one wants to versus doing a good job because one promised to are two very different things. It turns out that the evidence suggests both are important.

Another strand of the literature features multiple-preference and utility models. For instance, in *Selfishness, Altruism, and Rationality,* Howard Margolis (1982) offers a model in which individuals get two irreducible kinds of utility from two different kinds of preferences: private and social. Self-interested acts fulfill one kind of preference, altruistic acts another kind. Innovatively, Margolis formulates a rule, operationalized as a weight, that gives the ratio of spending in each category of preference necessary to result in an equilibrium. That weight, in turn, is subject to Darwinian evolutionary forces. Evolution selects not for those who are narrowly self-interested but instead for those individuals who also participate in groups. Of course that is a very different kind of account than one that relies on conscious reflection and commitment to principles, but in any case the multiple-preference and utility literature will be briefly assessed in chapter 3.[18]

18. Along somewhat different lines from Margolis, but in line with the arguments in this book, Amitai Etzioni, in *The Moral Dimension* (1988), offered an influential framework in which individuals are motivated by both moral principles and self-interested preferences. Etzioni takes a "moderately deontological" position with respect to moral acts: their rightness stems mostly from an individual's intent, not the estimated outcome. Ultimately, however, Etzioni conceptualizes such moral motivations in terms of moral *preferences.*

If my explanation for why people would tell the truth in economic interactions differs from that of economists, so does it differ for why people would lie. For instance, in *Private Truths, Public Lies* Timur Kuran (1995) suggests that people sometimes engage in preference falsification, a type of lie in which one misrepresents her true motivation or disposition in order to manipulate the perceptions of others. For instance, such a person might disingenuously feign a private preference in public in order to enhance her reputation. In contrast, for those who might otherwise be tempted to act with commitment-integrity, lying stems more from a failure to choose moral principles, weakness of will, errors in judgment, self-deception, or moral exclusion. Moreover, and once again, we largely focus on different contexts. Kuran looks at scenarios where social pressure might induce one to conform against one's true preferences (e.g., revealing one's true political views). Since the topic of this book is economic agreements, the social pressure of fidelity would most often reinforce the behavior one promised in the first place.

The organization of the book is straightforward, beginning with the development of the theory. Chapter 2 introduces preference-integrity, sketches a simple framework, and assesses its strengths and weaknesses. Chapter 3 does the same for commitment-integrity, but since the concept is more of a departure, the chapter also goes into some depth to include its philosophical and psychological foundations. This chapter provides the core theoretical foundation for the book. Chapter 4 considers game theory and social dilemmas. The mathematical analysis in these chapters is simple, to keep the analysis as accessible as possible.

Each of the four chapters that follow explores a different kind of agreement. Chapter 5 first goes into some detail about the notions of lying and mutual deceit in order to provide a solid foundation for the minimalist principle. The chapter then considers two different kinds of agreements, legal and political. Chapter 6 considers the very important employment agreement. As I alluded to earlier, the existence of workers of integrity is particularly consequential for both actual firms and also the literatures on the theory of the firm. Chapter 7 considers religious agreements and behavior. Religious principles are included, which necessitates investigating other issues, such as multiple identities. The chapter provides an example for what happens when we move beyond the minimalist principle. Chapter 8 investigates the normative requirement for a person of integrity who embraces only the minimalist principle, vis-à-vis human rights, a particular kind of social agreement. The role of coherence is particularly important here, and it provides the basis for thinking that persons of integrity have reason to support human rights.

Assuming that integrity is something people value, the question then becomes how it could be fostered. Chapter 9 addresses that psychological question with a four-part decision-making framework by specifically considering moral training and moral leadership. Finally, chapter 10 summarizes the thesis, addresses some remaining objections, and considers how integrity might rank with other dispositions worth valuing. While I try to anticipate the skeptics' criticisms throughout, in this last chapter I address the concerns of a perhaps more sympathetic audience—feminists and others, who might claim that the analysis here does not leave enough room for dispositions like emotions or caring.

The kind of integrity considered in this book is not particularly special. That's one reason why it merits further study. To achieve that goal, I will occasionally motivate chapters by deploying our friends Don Quixote and Volpone to illustrate opposite ends of the spectrum. To stand in for an ordinary person in the swirl of the complex middle, I will place Martha. Martha finds herself to be a party to different kinds of economic agreements that require decisions. Does she follow the dictates of integrity, or the tug and pull of her countervailing preferences?

Chapter 2

Preference-Integrity

Some people do not *like* to lie. Some people *really* do not like to lie. Others may be indifferent toward acts of lying, or may even like to lie, especially if doing so can help them achieve other objectives. But to the extent that we model lying, we tend to focus more on the consequences of a lie on other preferences or constraints. For example, a lie may increase one's consumption possibilities now but reduce them in the future if it hurts her reputation. In these kinds of analyses, one contractual party can trust another only because any violation of that trust will lead to unacceptable future losses. One is honest *because* that kind of behavior leads to the best material outcome for one's self. In contrast, in this chapter I will introduce *preference-integrity,* which is really nothing other than a strong preference for not lying. But we will see that even this simple version can generate novel implications.

First, a review of utility theory may be useful.

2.1. Utility Theory

Economists developed utility theory to describe and model economic decision making.[1] The starting point for utility theory is preferences. Each individual is assumed to possess preferences over all possible consumption bundles. These preferences enable comparisons, so any bundle can be judged relative to another. If five technical assumptions are fulfilled—namely, that preferences are complete, reflexive, transitive, continuous, and strongly monotonic—then it can be shown that a utility function exists that represents those preferences. Utility functions assign values to any consumption possi-

1. Most economists and students with advanced microeconomics training can just skim this section.

bility, with higher values representing preferred consumption opportunities relative to less preferred options.

The five technical assumptions on preferences merit brief comment, particularly in relation to different notions of rationality used by economists. Completeness means that individuals can evaluate all alternatives. Reflexivity means that any bundle is judged to be at least as good as itself. Transitivity requires individuals to be consistent in their choices. If bundle *A* is preferred to bundle *B*, which is in turn preferred to bundle *C*, then transitivity requires the individual to prefer *A* to *C*. Some evidence suggests that this assumption is not robust because people may violate it according to how alternatives are framed. But, taken together, these first three assumptions on preferences connote the formal definition of rationality for many economists.[2]

Other economists include strong monotonicity and the standard behavioral postulate of self-interest to define rationality. Strong monotonicity, or nonsatiation, simply means that more is preferred to less (a weaker version says that more is at least as good as less).[3] Economists often confine preferences to material goods, services, and leisure, so nonsatiation means that individuals judge themselves to be better off the more of these things they have. This assumption turns out to be important if we want to include the possibility of nonmaterial preferences (like honesty, for instance).

By themselves, the axioms on preferences do not describe how an individual will choose among different alternatives. An individual could prefer *A* to *B*, but choose *B* according to some other consideration. Therefore, the behavioral theory is closed with the assumption of self-interest. This assumption means that individuals choose *in order to* satisfy their own preferences. Since economists assume that individuals choose in such a way to maximize their preference satisfaction, this expanded version of rationality says that individuals are rational if they maximize their own utility. This kind of rationality is called *instrumental rationality.*

Why do economists feel most comfortable using material preferences, and "reasonable" ones at that? Nothing in the theory requires it; indeed, individuals could be assumed to have preferences over anything from altruism to revenge to eating sand. The reason economists eschew widespread inclusion is that otherwise any choice could be explained by a corresponding preference.

2. See, for instance, Jehle and Reny 1998, 112.

3. Continuity is a technical assumption greatly aiding the mathematical analysis, permitting the use of calculus on utility functions, for instance. It says that if bundle *A′* is strictly preferred to *B*, and if bundle *A* is sufficiently close to *A*, then *A′* is preferred to *B*.

Robert Frank calls this the "crankcase oil" problem.[4] Someone who drinks crankcase oil and then keels over and dies must have really liked crankcase oil. By including any conceivable preference, any behavior can be tautologically explained by claiming a preference for it. For economists, once a preference is posited and put into a utility function, that preference becomes the *reason* for behavior. It seems too simple and also strangely against one's own interests to do something for another just because of some kind of altruistic preference. At the very least economists try to first rule out other motives like reciprocity or reputation building that would further one's own material interests. For many economists, altruistic preferences are not necessary to explain seemingly utility-reducing current actions that return higher rewards later. It appears less tautological to explain such an act without reference to altruistic preferences.

One other feature about preferences stands out. At least for modeling purposes, economists assume that preferences are exogenously determined. That means that individuals do not have control over the preferences they are endowed with. If I am born with a taste for Mexican food, I do not intentionally try to change this taste, nor do I try to cultivate it.[5] Rather, I consider it a fact about my desires. I just need to evaluate the strength of that preference relative to my other preferences. The biggest reason we make this assumption is that it allows us to come up with determinate solutions in choice problems. Along with prices and income (and skills), it represents the starting point. If preferences were not already given, economists would have to find their determinants—to open the "black box," if you will. Most economists feel the starting point a good one and believe it is a better division of labor to leave the origins of preferences to the other social sciences (e.g., sociology, psychology, anthropology). However, as we will see, some economists have challenged this assumption, and those pioneering efforts have created the room necessary for the kind of analysis offered in this book.[6]

Utility theory is finally closed with the consumer's constraint. Most people would like to indulge their most luxurious tastes, at least once in awhile, but often do not. Consumers possess limited income to allocate among their consumption alternatives, each of which comes at a price deter-

4. Frank 1997a, 215.

5. There are exceptions. For instance, heterodox economist John Davis does include the possibility of cultivating tastes in his account of the individual in economics (2003).

6. Galbraith (1958) challenged the exogeneity assumption many years back. He argued that the efforts of marketers to change consumer preferences toward their products meant that welfare analyses on the attributes of the market were severely compromised.

mined in the market. As mentioned earlier, from the consumer's point of view, prices and income are also taken as given. (Actually, income is the result of another choice problem about labor supply, which in turn is determined by exogenously determined preferences on leisure versus labor, skills, and wage options.) The individual's problem then is to allocate her income across her consumption opportunities in way that maximizes her utility (or preference satisfaction), given preferences, prices, and income. This characterization determines a unique consumption choice; that is the theory's supreme virtue, that it gives a solution to the choice problem individuals confront. And, by calculating the consumer's response to different prices, demand curves can be derived.

One problem sometimes mentioned about utility theory is that it is based on preferences, which by their very nature are unobservable. In contrast, the choices made by individuals often are observable. So, based on utility theory, economists begin with something we can't observe to make predictions about something we can.

Nobel laureate Paul Samuelson offered a different approach, that of revealed preferences. For Samuelson and followers of his approach, assumptions are made about consistency of choices themselves, such that inferences can be made about the preferences that caused those choices. If one consumption bundle is chosen over another that is equally available, the individual has a revealed preference for the first over the second. The Strong Axiom of Revealed Preference rules out intransitive revealed preferences, quite analogously to the transitivity assumption on preferences, which implies that a utility function exists that represents observed behavior. Then the issue becomes one of recovering the actual utility function. Data limitations may make the task difficult but certainly not theoretically impossible.

Efforts like the revealed preference approach and utility theory itself were largely devised as a way of testing the implications of utility theory, particularly those of consumer demand. Consumer demand involves choices of material goods and services. Perhaps that is why economists have been most comfortable with material preferences. But while economists have been reluctant to posit particular preferences so as to avoid the appearance of tautology, there are some prominent exceptions, like those mentioned in chapter 1. These kinds of modeling strategies are permissible if they are done carefully and selectively, and especially if they can generate nontrivial implications that are not initially accessible to our intuition. Modeling integrity as a preference that people hold meets these requirements.

2.2. Preference-Integrity

There are two common meanings associated with everyday usage of the term *integrity*. One is wholeness: "the quality of state of being complete or undivided: material, spiritual, or aesthetic wholeness." The other involves a moral sense: "an uncompromising adherence to a code of moral, artistic, or other values: utter sincerity, honesty, and candor"[7] or "soundness of moral principle; the character of uncorrupted virtue, esp. in relation to truth and fair dealing; uprightness, honesty, sincerity."[8] A minimalist interpretation of a person of integrity is that such a person is honest. To be sure, it can mean more or something a bit different as I will describe in the next chapter, but honesty is the most common meaning people attribute to the term.

For economists then, to describe a person of integrity would be to posit a strong or decisive preference of honesty to that person. If the preference were strong enough, the person's choices would reflect telling the truth or not lying, no matter what the person's other desires or preferences. That is, this type of person would choose an honest act if that act maximized her preference satisfaction (utility) more expeditiously than the available options.[9] I call this type of integrity *preference-integrity*. Note that this concept is faithful to economic methodology, even if it does require a mild leap of faith for those economists who don't typically embrace nonmaterial preferences.[10]

To better understand the idea, consider it more formally. Let $\mathbf{x} = x_1, \ldots, x_n$ represent all of the n acts an individual could undertake. They represent acts of consumption, effort provision, and some act based on honesty. Let x_1 be that act, not lying in order to increase some other material payoff, say. For simplicity, assume that x_1 is a dichotomous variable, taking the value of 0 for an honest act not taken and 1 for an honest act taken. This assumption will be relaxed in chapter 4, where a simple game-theoretic model is introduced. Otherwise, the individual has preference relations following the assumptions mentioned in the last section. These relationships are preserved and described with a utility function $U(x_1, \ldots, x_n)$ that, among other things, measures the individual's level of well-being, in this case preference satisfaction, for any

7. *Webster's Third International Dictionary, Unabridged.*

8. *Oxford English Dictionary*, 2d ed.

9. For another preference account of morality, see Dowell, Goldfarb, and Griffith 1998.

10. One colleague has commented to me that some agents may cultivate a disposition for honesty because then it would either reduce the cost of signaling that beneficial disposition, or because it would reduce the probability of costly memory lapses. The response is that were it in the agent's power to develop an honest disposition, it would really not be any different than the preference for honesty I will soon describe.

given values of $x_1, \ldots, x_n$. Recall that for both the individual being described and for the researcher modeling the individual's behavior, preferences are exogenous, or outside of the system of analysis. It will be useful to make the stronger assumption that the utility function is *cardinal,* meaning that given measures can be compared proportionally. If some values of $\mathbf{x}$ give utility of z, and some other $\mathbf{x}'$ gives utility of $2z$, we can say that the individual is exactly twice as well off in the latter case.

For each x_i there is an associated price, p_i. For the moment we suppress x_1, as it is not typically included in economic analysis. The individual has income y and spends it all if $p_2x_2 + \ldots + p_ix_i + \ldots + p_nx_n = y$, which is the individual's constraint. Given the utility function and the constraint, the individual maximizes utility by choosing $\mathbf{x}^*$ such that $U_2/p_2 = \ldots = U_i/p_i = \ldots = U_n/p_n$, where $U_i = \partial U/\partial x_i$—the marginal (or additional) utility of x_i.[11] This famous maximization rule just says that the individual should choose acts such that the marginal utility of each act per dollar spent is equalized. Since the price of any good is its marginal cost, the utility maximization rule can also be interpreted to say that the individual should choose such that the marginal benefit to marginal cost ratio is equalized for all x_i. The constraint assures that the individual's choices are bounded.

Preference-integrity is modeled as follows. Since it requires that the preference for honesty is decisive, the marginal utility at $x_1 = 1$ must be quite high, approaching some arbitrarily high value. Thus U_1/p_1 takes on a high value that cannot be matched by any other U_i/p_i. In such a case, the person of preference-integrity chooses $x_1 = 1$, and then the remaining $x_2, \ldots, x_n$ such that $U(1, \ldots, x_n)$ is maximized subject to the constraint $p_2x_2 + \ldots + p_ix_i + \ldots + p_nx_n = y - p_1x_1$. The solution to that problem is $(1, x_2^*, \ldots, x_n^*)$. Note that while it may not have an explicit price, acting honestly can reduce income. But the person of preference-integrity chooses to act honestly because of the decisive preference and then allocates her remaining income in the standard way. Honest behavior results from a direct preference for honesty, not some other instrumental motive. There is nothing fancy about modeling such behavior.[12]

It turns out that preference-integrity can nontrivially explain a lot of real-life economic behavior. Typically, when an economic agent says that she will keep an agreement or perform an act that otherwise appears to be against her material interests, and it costs the agent nothing (again, materially) to lie,

11. We usually assume that U_i is positive but decreasing with increases in x_i. Eating the first burrito increases my welfare more than the second one.

12. The discontinuity of x_1 is a little tricky but is in fact very similar to how Dowell, Goldfarb, and Griffith (1998) model honesty. Also see the notion of strong sympathy in Minkler 1999.

economists refer to such representations as "cheap talk" or "hot air," meaning they are not to be believed. Contracts and economic arrangements are structured so as to make cheap talk irrelevant by introducing appropriate incentives and penalties for nonperformance. But, as mentioned in chapter 1, the evidence suggests that such representations are often kept and are sincere even in the absence of incentives or penalties.

2.3. An Assessment of Preference-Integrity

Two primary virtues stand out in the assessment of preference-integrity. First, since preference-integrity is really nothing more than a strongly held preference, albeit a nonmaterial one, the theory is well worked out. Essentially, an agent will act on a moral preference if the additional benefits of doing so exceed the additional costs. A strongly held moral preference means that the benefits of associated acts are high and thus more likely to be undertaken. For example, a person of preference-integrity does not want to keep the proceeds of an undercharge because the utility of the increased cash is not as great as the utility loss from dishonesty. If preferences, prices, and a few other things are known, quite precise predictions could be made because the theory is so well developed. Even if exact preferences are not known, revealed-preference theory could generate a fair number of implications based on observed choices.

The second virtue, I think, relates to methodological realism. It is virtuous for a theory to start from assumptions that accurately describe reality. And it certainly seems true that at least some moral dispositions could best be described as *preferences*. Many experimenters interpret evidence of the type discussed in chapter 1, especially those experiments that find reciprocating behavior, as resulting from preferences.[13] Also, often people clearly do act out

13. Some evolutionary psychologists conjecture that such dispositions arose because they confer an evolutionary advantage (e.g., Cosmides and Tooby 1994). The idea is that people prefer to reciprocate because that kind of behavior more expeditiously solves problems than other kinds of behavior. Our hominid ancestors who cooperated were more likely to obtain food and fend off predators than those who behaved selfishly. Because they got more resources and were more likely to live and see another day, the genes of those who cooperated were more likely to achieve genetic propagation. This "selfish gene" underlies cooperative, or reciprocating, preferences. This notion has its critics, including Robin Dawes and his coauthors who interpret their experimental results of in-group bias as arising from the rival evolutionary theory of "sociality" (Caporael, Dawes, Orbell, and van de Kragt 1989). Perhaps just as important, Prisoner's Dilemma, Public Goods, Dictator, and Ultimatum game experiments have really not been designed in a way that can decisively identify the reasons for observed cooperative behavior. Experimenters often *assume* the existence of some kind of cooperative preference and then speculate about its origin. But as we will see in the next

of self-interest. Thus it would not be odd for someone to say that they are honest because they want to be, and beyond that they haven't thought about it much or even think they needed to. Preference-integrity describes such a person. It is important to emphasize that this person acts honestly because it is in her interest to do so. While that may seem on the surface too selfish, in many instances we probably would not want it any other way. We tend to want people to *want* to do the right thing as opposed to just blindly following their perceived obligations. Certainly in our personal relationships we want others to be honest with us because they truly want to be, not simply because they feel obligated to do so.

Perhaps the primary weakness with a preference-based account of integrity is that it can't accommodate coherence, or the unity of character. The topic of coherence will be addressed in detail in the next chapter on commitment-integrity, however, there is nothing in the conceptualization of preference-integrity that would rule out a person with a strong preference for honesty who also has a strong preference to steal from or to harm others. Nothing rules out lying to right-handed but not to left-handed people. In utility theory, preferences are determined exogenously, and there really is no provision (yet) for disqualifying seemingly morally contradictory preferences.

There are four other features of utility theory, and thus preference-integrity, that are also problematic. Utility theory is (1) reductionist, (2) self-referential, (3) instrumental, and (4) deterministic. *Reductionism* means that all of that which the agent values can be described by preferences of varying intensity.[14] It might seem that it could not be otherwise. But, as Amartya Sen has famously explicated, commitments are different from preferences because the former can drive a wedge between personal choice and personal welfare.[15] Commitments are rules imposed on oneself (as opposed to external constraints), and are the result of conscious deliberation. They take the form of personal imperatives in that the agent reasons that they must or mustn't do such and such. Since commitments exist but cannot be differentiated from preferences in utility theory, that constitutes a departure from methodological realism.

Utility theory is also self-referential in the sense that any reason for action

chapter, such behavior could also arise from individuals consciously reflecting about and then choosing moral *principles*. Even if they choose to act on their preferences, that too could stem from conscious reflection. In any case, that insight implies that the experimental results could derive from either preferences, other evolutionary factors like sociality, commitments to principles, or any combination.

14. See Sen and Williams 1982; Harcourt 1998.

15. Sen 1978.

has to make reference to the agent's own welfare, and particularly how it is to be maximized. If alternatives *A* and *B* are equally available, and the agent chooses *A*, it must have been that *A* yielded higher welfare to the agent. It is important to emphasize that even if *A* is something that benefits another, the reason the agent took the action was to increase her own welfare. The great traditions of moral philosophy (perhaps apart from Hume) and religion subscribe to the notion that moral acts are either right or they fulfill the good without referencing the individual's interests. If these traditions are correct, then preference-integrity is fundamentally at odds with reasons for moral behavior, and no matter whatever its other strengths are, it is not morally virtuous.[16]

Utility theory is instrumental in the following sense.[17] Since the highest-order objective of an economic agent is to maximize her own welfare, any action taken serves this final purpose. We all have desires. In economics they are represented by preferences. But in principle just because we have desires does not mean that we have to act on them. Something further is needed to determine how we will include our desires in making choices. In utility theory the behavior postulate is to maximize our own welfare, which means preference satisfaction or desire fulfillment. Therefore, our highest desire is to fulfill our desires. Among other things, that means if I help you, I do so in order to achieve *my* final objective, which is to fulfill my desires; as such, you are an instrument to me.[18] If I am a person of preference-integrity and I am honest

16. This is especially so because even if one could base a truly moral account on desire-based reasons it would have to be the case that one's desires are brought into line with moral actions judged to be correct. There is no mechanism in utility theory and hence preference-integrity for such judgments or alignments. See Foot 1972, reprinted in Darwall et al. 1997, along with her recantation of externalist reasons.

17. See Minkler 1999.

18. On this basis Martin Buber (1958) anticipates economic man objectifying others in I-It rather than I-Thou relations. The contrasting view redirects the focus to the objects of desire themselves (see Darwall 1983, 37, in his criticism of desire-based reasons). That is, it is our preferences that define our goals. In that case, if I help you it is both my desire and my objective; there is no higher objective, and hence you are not an instrument for me to increase my welfare. Stated differently, it is not our (increased) welfare we seek, but rather that which increases our welfare. While that view may have merit in some contexts, it does not represent utility theory. Utility theory starts with conditions on preferences over objects and experiences but ends up with the decisions being made in a way that allows comparability and ranking of all desires and objectives in order that final personal welfare can be maximized. The ultimate locus is one's own personal desire to fulfill one's own desires. To illustrate, suppose you see someone you don't know in distress. If you help her, did it stem simply and completely from the desire to help her as Darwall describes? Maybe, but that is not how an economist using utility theory would describe it. On that account you would help the person because it gave you the pleasant experience of a warm glow, or because it reduced your own discomfort of inaction. Either way, the final motivation lay with maximizing your own welfare.

with you, then I am using you to fulfill my preference for honesty. That is to say, you are a means to my higher desired end.

Finally, utility theory and preference-integrity are deterministic in the sense that behavior is caused by factors completely outside of the individual's control. Determinism is the opposite of autonomy, which means free of external causes. In determinism, everything relevant is outside of the individual's control, especially preferences. Preferences are exogenously *given to the individual* in utility theory. They are given by God, nature, or maybe social forces in more recent formulations.[19] The advantage of a deterministic theory is that it allows researchers to find deterministic solutions, given the proper data. The disadvantage is that it does not permit truly free choice by individuals. One implication of a deterministic theory is that if agents are accurately described and behave in such a manner they could not be held responsible for their actions.[20] The notion of moral responsibility would be meaningless. For instance, if an individual lies, others will typically judge the behavior as wrong. But lying could only be wrong if the offending individual had a choice in the matter, that is, if only he could be responsible for his own actions. Economic man has no such power because he did not choose his preference to lie or his preference to otherwise benefit from the lie. Given this limitation in utility theory, the only judgment that could be rendered from an economist's perspective is whether the lie was rational or not.

19. Efforts to endogenize preferences like those of evolutionary game theory still see preferences as outside of the individual's control. Instead, preferences are endogenous to the environment or economic or social system. Those efforts will be discussed in more detail in chapter 4.

20. Philosophers consider the issue to be more complex than this characterization. The position I'm describing is that of "incompatibilists," who believe that determinism would negate moral responsibility. In contrast, "compatibilists" believe that determinism does not negate freedom and hence moral responsibility. However, they attribute a peculiar meaning to freedom, in that alternative choices are never taken.

Chapter 3

Commitment-Integrity

For many, the shortcomings of preference-integrity will suggest the need for a rendering more faithful to the way we usually think about integrity. The version in this chapter addresses that concern by introducing the notion of *commitment-integrity,* which, most fundamentally, features conscious reflection on principles, a commitment to those chosen, and the will. Don Quixote, perhaps unrealistically, commits to the moral principle of correcting every wrong, and he possesses indomitable will that allows him to act accordingly. Volpone consciously chooses unflinchingly to fulfill his own preferences, whatever they might be. Martha is more conflicted. She accepts the truth of some principles and even commits to them, but sometimes her preferences conflict with those principles, and her will is not unshakable. She is therefore confronted with the problem of how to decide between her principles and her preferences, a position many will empathize with. Conceptualizing that decision process is the topic of this chapter.

3.1. Commitment-Integrity

Preference-integrity captures an important moral element of integrity, namely, honesty as a disposition. There are at least two other important elements to consider. First, there is the notion of wholeness, which relates to the person's character or identity. Second, there is the person's relation to moral values. Integrity is usually thought to require that a person *choose* moral principles for herself and then make them her own. The definition of integrity offered by the *Oxford Companion to Philosophy* (1995) makes these aspects especially clear.

> The quality of a person who can be counted upon to give precedence to moral considerations, even when there is strong inducement to let

> self-interest or some claimant desire override them, or where the betrayal of moral principle might pass undetected. To have integrity is to have unconditional and steady commitment to moral values and obligations. For such a person, the fundamental question of whether to conduct life on the plane of self-concern or of moral seriousness has been decisively resolved, though particular life situations will doubtless continue to put that commitment to strenuous test. This moral commitment becomes a crucial component in his or her sense of identity as a person; it confers a unity (integration) of character, and even a simplicity upon the man or woman of integrity. What integrity cannot guarantee is the soundness of the value-judgements themselves, which form the core of that person's commitments.

Many philosophers have offered thoughtful accounts of integrity—its features, normative requirements, and implications—including Bernard Williams, Gabriele Taylor, Mark Halfon, and Jeffry Blustein.[1] Philosopher Lynne McFall offers a particularly good account of what integrity requires.[2] McFall differentiates personal from moral integrity: the former requires a person to commit to identity-conferring principles; the latter adds the further requirement that the principles must also be moral. An artist who commits to art for its own sake is an example of a person of personal integrity. Bernard Williams is even more inclusive. In offering a famous argument on why utilitarianism precludes personal integrity he suggests, "One can be committed to such things as a person, a cause, an institution, a career, one's own genius, or the pursuit of danger."[3] But in McFall's account, a person of integrity is one who embraces a coherent set of commitments to principles that, when taken together, confer identity to the person. The stress on principles is important because principles are usually universal or impartial. As we will see, that feature plays an important role in the notion of coherence, and its lapses.

Commitments, personal imperatives or internal constraints, must become one's own; one cannot have an impersonal relation to identity-conferring commitments. For a person to violate her identity-conferring commitment, then, would mean for her to lose her identity.[4] Utterances like "I could

1. Smart and Williams 1973; Taylor 1971; Halfon 1989; Blustein 1991.
2. McFall 1987.
3. Smart and Williams 1973, 112. Williams argues that utilitarianism subordinates anyone's own personal projects in favor of social welfare–increasing actions, which makes the idea of integrity impossible. As a logical matter, the criticism is wrong, at least for some conceptual cases. As Jeffrey Blustein (1991, chapter 6) points out, if one adopts as her own central personal project to maximize social welfare, then integrity and utilitarianism can be consistent with one another.
4. In what follows, I will not differentiate identity from self-conception and will in fact use them synonymously. A deeper analysis of identity would treat it as a relation where the self takes the self

not live with myself if I did that" reflect the link between identity and certain commitments.[5] Coherence refers to the aspect of integrity associated with integral wholeness. Coherence requires consistency between one's motivation and principles, consistency among one's commitments, and consistency among one's actions and commitments. For instance, committing to truth-telling but also to thievery would be incoherent, as would committing to only truth-telling in principle but lying in practice.

McFall further argues that a person maximizing her own welfare could not be a person of integrity because then there could never be the possibility of a conflict between doing what one wants and what one is committed to. The possibility of that conflict and choosing in favor of commitment instead of self-interest are necessary conditions for the existence of integrity.

What McFall's account does not provide is how an individual could (1) choose among different principles and (2) transform chosen principles into acts. McFall provides the requirements of identity-conferring commitments and coherence without really offering an account of the individual's decision process that could meet those requirements. Those questions have been more the focus of philosophers who seek to understand the normative requirements of rationality.

The work of Christine Korsgaard is particularly instructive and provides the basis for much of what follows.[6] Korsgaard's aim is to provide a rational basis for moral obligations. She argues that there are certain moral principles that the agent *must* accept. Her analysis is explicitly Kantian in that certain maxims are good based upon their internal structure, that is, they are fit to be willed as universal law.[7] Rather than analyzing what principles the agent *should* hold, my more modest purpose is to understand *how* the agent comes to accept moral principles and what happens when the agent *does* accept certain moral principles. The following gives a brief account of the reflective nature of the mind, and the associated functions of identity, social influences, and the will.

The first task is to understand how an individual could make a judgment about moral principles. To make a judgment is to come to a belief; but what is one to believe if confronted with potentially conflicting moral principles, other kinds of principles, and desires? One *has to* choose, which means one

---

as object (see Davis 2003). While not discussing integrity directly, Jencks 1990 provides an interesting account of how individuals come to include other persons, communities, and moral ideals in their personal notions of self.

5. Korsgaard (1994, 393) makes this point in reference to obligations.

6. Korsgaard 1994.

7. Korsgaard 1994, 394.

can choose. The ability to choose derives from the self-conscious nature of the human mind. The mind not only perceives thoughts, some of which are about moral principles, ideas, and desires, but much like Adam Smith's impartial spectator, it also knows that it perceives those contents and can step back and evaluate and reflect upon them. This distance means that individuals are not hostage to the mind's contents. If a desire arises, one does not immediately have to act on it. Just because a thought or an idea presents itself does not mean that we have to accept it or believe it to be true. Aristotle said as much; so do Buddhists. Instead, rational agents scrutinize the mind's contents and sift through its elements, deciding what to accept. These thoughts, ideas, and desires that are ultimately accepted represent reflective successes, or reasons to act. According to Kant, rational agents not only can choose but can (and must) choose freely among the mind's contents presented to them by virtue of free will—one that is self-determining.[8]

As we will see in section 3.5 on psychological foundations, this philosophical account of conscious reflection rests on a certain cognitive process. But it's worth interjecting here that neuroscientists generally support the role of reason in decision making. In fact the aim of recent research is to show that human decisions are not the sole product of reason, that emotions can also play a role. To do so, neuroscientists have sought to locate the brain mechanisms associated with decision making. Some evidence suggests that the decisions of those with damage to their ventromedial prefrontal cortex are inferior in both quality and speed.[9] The idea is that that kind of brain damage reduces one's emotional capacity, which in turn reduces one's anticipatory response prior to a decision. Roughly, if an individual cannot anticipate how she will feel as a result of any given decision, it will be more difficult for her to make a good, timely decision in the first place.[10]

Neuroscientists have also studied the decision-making properties of "normal" brains with technologies like functional magnetic resonance imaging (fMRI), a technique that measures local blood concentration levels. For instance, in one study participants were asked to respond to three different kinds of dilemmas.[11] In the first, a personal moral dilemma, participants were asked to contemplate a situation where they could inflict direct harm on an-

8. In fact, Kant argued that rational persons possess a free will and as such can recognize and are obligated to choose the moral law (1785).

9. See, for instance, Bechara and Damasio 2005.

10. The fuller theory relies on somatic markers, or signals that arise in bioregulatory processes. Since the theory further relies on a particular kind of (reinforcement) learning process, Elster (1998, 63) believes that the theory provides a persuasive correlative, but not causal, link between somatic markers and decisions.

11. See Cohen 2005.

other in order to prevent harm to a greater number. For instance, they could choose to kill a person on train tracks so as to block a runaway railcar from killing an even larger number. In the second, an impersonal moral dilemma, they could inflict incidental harm on another to prevent greater harm. For instance, they could pull a switch to divert the runaway train, quite unfortunately for a hapless bystander who happened to be standing on the diverted track. The third was a nonmoral dilemma requiring a similar degree of mental effort. The researchers found that the areas of the brain that were activated among the participants confronted with the first dilemma were those associated with emotional responses, like the medial frontal cortex. In the second and third dilemmas, areas of the brain associated with abstract reasoning (the dorsolateral areas of the prefrontal cortex) were activated. Researchers interpret this kind of evidence as suggesting that while higher-level cognitions are usually responsible for deciding, sometimes emotions can influence our deliberative reasoning.[12]

So the mind can choose, but the question then becomes, how and what will it choose? Such choices are inextricably linked to how one views oneself—one's own identity.[13] The principles and desires one chooses as candidates for reasons for action are expressive of who one thinks she is. Certain principles and desires are associated with certain identities; certain identities are associated with certain principles and desires. If the reflective nature of consciousness chooses a particular identity, certain principles and desires become automatic candidates. One could choose to be an epicurean and attempt to indulge every refined desire that arises. One could choose to be an artist and live for art's own sake. Or one could choose an identity of moral integrity, which would then give the person reason to act on moral principles. Of course myriad potential identities exist, and other factors also enter into identity formation such as the groups one associates with, as in religious affiliations (the topic of chapter 7). Succinctly, the point is that choices can and do occur and that identity plays a central organizational role.

While the reflective nature of consciousness selects identities and desires and principles to act upon, it can only choose among those apprehended by the mind. The mind's contents therefore constrain those candidates for reflective successes. It is here that society and culture play a role because they in large part inform the mind's contents. Children initially learn social values

12. Of course some decisions are completely determined by emotion, like raging anger in the case of violence. The contexts for which those emotions would dominate are not really the subject of this book.

13. In addition to Davis (2003), economists who have recently looked at the notion of identity include Akerlof and Kranston (2000, 2005).

and customs from their caregivers, and then from an ever-expanding circle of social groups. Maturing adults learn about different kinds of behaviors, different reasons for behavior, and the personal and social consequences of choosing different courses of action.[14] Social situations crucially influence our menu of choices, as well as their potential costs and benefits.

Conditioned on its apprehended information, the reflective nature of consciousness requires acceptance of certain principles, desires, and identities. Each acceptance gives the agent reason, though not necessarily the compelling one, to act. Once the primary reason is chosen, it is now the will's turn to effectuate the act. The success of the will is not guaranteed—it may not be strong enough. But if a moral principle is accepted with which the agent identifies, and the agent successfully wills acts in accordance with that moral principle, then there exists reason for action.

How does integrity enter? While we know that identity-conferring commitments, the basis for commitment-integrity, are all internally imposed constraints, we can now say more—they derive from the reflective nature of consciousness's recognition and acceptance of certain moral principles. The chosen principles must be consistent with each other and with the chosen identity. The acts willed must also accord with those principles. This is the coherence referred to by McFall. Moral integrity thus requires an acceptance of moral principles, that these commitments are made one's own, and the necessary will to act upon those principles. Failure to accept, choose, or will to act upon moral principles (in the face of desire, say) is inconsistent with moral integrity. We may say that the person of moral integrity has reason to choose in a manner prescribed by the accepted principles.

To illustrate commitment-integrity and to differentiate it from a preference-based description of behavior, consider an example. Suppose Martha witnesses a muscular-looking man severely beating a child.[15] She has a clear preference against that state of affairs. The question now becomes, does she act, and if so, why? In case 1, if Martha attempts to stop the beating she may have reasoned that even though there is some likelihood that she herself will get hurt, an outcome she certainly doesn't desire, she fears the prospective pain she is likely to receive less than the discomfort (e.g., guilt or regret) she will feel if she doesn't make the attempt. Martha may try to take the action that minimizes her discomfort at the margin. But that is only one possible scenario for her decision process. In case 2, she may just as easily have rea-

14. See Boyd and Richerson 1990 for a good evolutionary account of the enculturation process.

15. Philosophers in particular love these type of examples. While it may seem morbid, it is perhaps tame compared to Sen's example of torture and Williams's example of (potentially mass) Indian murder.

soned that the state of affairs violated a moral principle she holds to be true and accepts, namely, "harming innocent children is wrong," and this acceptance constitutes a commitment such that she must act and shall do so if her will is sufficiently strong.[16] Now her distaste for the beating and the prospective guilt for not acting are certainly known to her but were not the primary reasons for her act. In fact, even in the first case the reason for her act was not fully spelled out. Martha's consideration of preference trade-offs presumed that she had already accepted and endorsed the "principle" that her act would be determined by her own welfare (i.e., her ultimate desire being to fulfill her desires most expeditiously).

So the big difference between a preference and a commitment is that a preference is self-referencing and subject to assessments against other preferences, while a commitment is an accepted and endorsed principle the agent sees she must act upon. If Martha identifies with the commitment of stopping harm against children, the prospective guilt she might feel if she did not attempt to do so would *not* be the decisive factor in her deliberation.[17]

We can now formalize commitment-integrity a bit. Based upon the preceding, the decision process for the person of commitment-integrity occurs in stages. First, the individual chooses what principles to identify with from the process of conscious reflection. Coherence requires that the principles chosen must be compatible with one another. Second, relevant acts are matched with relevant principles. If an act is judged to be relevant to a chosen principle, coherence further requires that the act be chosen. Third, since the act may not be chosen if the will to act is insufficient, a comparison is made between the strength of will and the difference between the utility of acting on the principle and not. The comparison determines if the act is chosen or not. Finally, the remaining income is spent according to the usual utility-maximizing procedure.

To model the first stage, the individual chooses among k different principles, denoted by $\pi_1 \ldots \pi_k$. The process of conscious reflection is endogenous to the individual, but exogenous to the researcher modeling commitment-integrity. That means that the individual chooses $\pi_1 \ldots \pi_k$ according to a process not predetermined by other causes that the researcher can model.[18] Once

16. Of course she is still aware of the potential impending harm, but her will is sufficiently strong to override her distaste for that harm.

17. See Harcourt 1998, 195.

18. Certainly there are factors that influence the choice such as one's cognitive development and reference groups, but because of a free (even if weak) will they are not causal and cannot be used to *determine* the principles chosen.

chosen, however, the researcher can take them as given data, just as she would preferences.

Once principles are chosen, they become reasons for acting. In the second stage the individual makes a judgment about which acts are relevant for the principles chosen. One principle could cover many different acts, and different principles could cover the same act. To keep matters simple, and to facilitate comparisons with preference-integrity, assume that the individual chooses only the minimalist principle, π_1, namely, "lying is wrong." Further assume that only one act, x_1, is relevant for the principle. Coherence requires that to adopt π_1 means to choose x_1.

Third, the individual assesses the strength of her exogenously determined will to act, given by the value μ. This value is commensurate with the individual's cardinal utility function. In particular, a comparison can be made between μ and $U(0, x_2, \ldots, x_n) - U(1, x_2, \ldots, x_n) = \Delta U$. At this stage, the individual is not trying to maximize utility, but rather to compare the utility difference between lying or not lying with the strength of the will to act. If the individual prefers not to lie, and if that preference overrides all other potential benefits, then ΔU is negative and the strength of the will to act is not important. But when the desire to lie yields otherwise positive net utility, the strength of the will to act is important. Specifically, if $\Delta U > \mu$ the individual cannot will the act. This possibility of incoherence, of course, increases with a strong desire to lie, and/or a weak will to act. So the individual chooses $x_1 = 1$ if $\Delta U < \mu$, 0 otherwise.

Finally, the individual spends the rest of her $y - p_1 x_1$ income by choosing $x_2, \ldots, x_n$ to maximize her utility.

Note that in deciding whether to choose an honest act or not, the person of commitment-integrity may confront a conflict between her desires and her identity-conferring commitments. The analysis captures this conflict, which has been described by philosophers through the ages, and more recently by psychologists. But that conflict is secondary in nature. Specifying the stages makes clear that the first and more fundamental problem for the individual is to choose her identity, or, what Thomas Wren calls self-interpretation.[19] That cognitive effort necessitates determining what is true and/or meaningful. It is logically prior to and thus influences the nature of the desire-commitment conflict. Until and unless the individual has made the effort to choose her identity, conflict with desires is irrelevant.

Therefore, based on the notions of preference-integrity and commitment-integrity, a person acts honestly in either of the two following condi-

19. See especially Wren 1991, 165.

tions: (1) if the individual has not chosen any principles, or has chosen the principle to fulfill her own desires, and if there is a decisive preference for honesty (e.g., $x_1 = 1$); or (2) if the individual chooses the principle of honesty (π_1), and opposing preferences do not override the will to act ($\Delta U < \mu$).[20]

3.2. Reasons

When philosophers look for justification and motivation for choice or action, they focus on *reasons*. This section uses those insights to examine the kinds of reasons employed by persons of both preference-integrity and commitment-integrity. The purpose is to further clarify the distinction between the two kinds of integrity.

In Davidson's (1963) pioneering analysis, the primary reason for an action derives from an agent's (1) pro-attitude and (2) belief about that action. *Pro-attitude* refers to some view or state of affairs to which the agent is favorably disposed. *Belief* refers to the agent's mental view that the action considered would bring about the intended state. Since the resulting action is independent of the primary reason, the latter can cause and thus explain the former. As an example, consider utility theory. The agent's pro-attitude is her ultimate desire to maximize her own welfare, and her belief is that choices ordered in such a way as to give primacy to highest utility per dollar spent will do so. Thus, while it is not usually framed this way by economists, it is correct to say, "the *reason* an agent chooses some act *B* is that it maximizes her utility (preference satisfaction)."[21]

This point is crucial. Clearly, utility maximization provides a reason for action, often a most powerful one. But it is only one possible reason. Economists usually assume, if only implicitly, that one's own maximal preference satisfaction is the only possible reason for acting. If behavior seems to deviate from material self-interest, then a nonmaterial preference is posited. The agent is always assumed to possess the pro-attitude toward self-interest, so the satisfaction of some preference then provides the reason for the behavior. All behavior is explained this way; any other deviations are deemed irrational.

20. As will be discussed in section 3.4, an individual may also fail to act with commitment-integrity if she makes a cognitive mistake, or if she suffers from self-deceit or moral exclusion, any of which could mean that she fails to recognize that π_1 implies $x_1 = 1$. Chapter 9, "On the Possibility of Integrity," discusses these issues in greater detail. Also note that the addition of expressive utility (Kuran 1995), which captures the need for self-assertion, would increase the likelihood of conditions (1) and (2) being fulfilled. In both cases one receives added utility from behaving honestly. Expressive utility will be considered further in the context of religious integrity, the topic of chapter 7.
21. Hausman and McPherson (2006 ch. 5) make a similar point.

If, however, it is recognized that agents could embrace a pro-attitude toward motives other than the primacy of their own desire satisfaction, then other reasons for action become readily available. For instance, a person of commitment-integrity has a pro-attitude toward the commitment to certain moral principles, and it is that disposition that underlies the different reason for action. The person of commitment-integrity also possesses preferences, but satisfying those preferences does not form the basis for the reason for acting.[22]

That individuals could choose moral actions independently, or somewhat independently, of their own desires and interests has been the focus of two different kinds of conceptions about reasons. The first, "practical reason," goes back to the Classical Greek era, while the second, "internal" versus "external" reasons, is a distinction developed and used more recently.

Practical reason derives from the notion (especially Aristotle's use of it) of *phronesis*, or practical wisdom. Practical reason is the ability to use intellect to make judgments, particularly ethical ones, according to rational standards, in practical matters. The *Oxford Companion to Philosophy* says that it is "a measure of disengagement from personal wish and want, a readiness to appraise one's acts by criteria which (rising above individual contingent desire) can be every rational moral agent's criteria, mark[ing] a crucial point of insertion of reason into practice." Another way of thinking about it would be to borrow from Davidson's framework. In that case, a reason deriving from practical reason would be a type of primary reason about which the pro-attitude was moral, or the result of moral deliberation. Practical reason, therefore, offers an alternative to the decision-making process of utility theory, in which the resulting reasons for action can have a moral, rather than personal, welfare-maximizing basis.

A more recent distinction concerns internalism versus externalism.[23] Internalists hold that reasons must refer to motivations, while externalists hold that reasons can refer to either justifications or motivations, and that the two are logically independent.[24] Internal reasons come in two stripes, one inspired by Kant, the other Hume. The first holds that the moral truth of propositions provides an intrinsic, or at least prima facie, motivation for acting. The sec-

22. Interestingly, Davidson is sometimes seen as suggesting that desire is the sole possible pro-attitude, but I find this reading too narrow (e.g., see Darwall 1983, 27). Davidson explicitly includes "a great variety of moral views" and "public views" as possible candidates for pro-attitude (1963, 686), as well as duties, obligations, and believing something to be right (689–90).

23. The term *internalism* was apparently introduced in Falk 1947–48.

24. Robertson and Stocker 1992. The authors provide perhaps the clearest account of this otherwise confusing and confused distinction.

ond, inspired more by Hume, says that a moral justification only becomes a reason if it is *also* desired by an agent. The desire is what motivates the agent to act, and the addition of the motivation is what makes it a reason. On this account, if there is moral justification but no desire, there is no reason to act.

Externalists, in contrast, separate justifying and motivating reasons. A compelling moral theory can justify a consideration for action. If it does so it is a justifying reason. But the motive for acting (motivating reason) can be an entirely separate reason. Unlike internalism, no necessary link between justification and motivation exists. Typically, desire often does provide the motivating reason for action, just like in Humean internalism, providing a source of considerable confusion. The two are different because Humean internalism holds that both justifications *and* motivations (desires) are necessary for reasons, while externalists hold that *either* sufficient justification *or* motivation constitutes a reason. What they have in common is that, unlike Kantian internalism, moral principles by themselves are not sufficient to motivate an agent to act.

Kantian internalism might be thought of as normatively referring to what rationality requires.[25] I take the term to refer to what the agent herself judges the moral requirement to be. This is how Thomas Nagel uses the term when he writes that the "presence of a motivation for acting morally is guaranteed by the truth of ethical propositions themselves. On this view the motivation must be so tied to the truth, or meaning, of ethical statements that when in a particular case some one is (*or perhaps merely believes he is*) morally required to do something, it follows that he has a motivation for doing it" (emphasis added).[26] Similarly, Christine Korsgaard writes, "An internalist theory is a theory according to which the knowledge (or truth *or acceptance*) of a moral judgment implies the existence of a motive (not necessarily overriding) for acting on that judgment" (emphasis added).[27] Practical reason, therefore, yields internalist reasons for acting. Such agents deliberate on the truth of moral propositions and, once accepted, develop a pro-attitude. Combined with the belief that associated acts will affect the morally prescribed state of affairs, the agent has the motivation or reason to engage in the acts quite apart from her other interests. This brief summary ties together reasons, practical reason, and (Kantian) internalism.

The account I have offered on preference-integrity can be said to be externalist, while the one offered on commitment-integrity is internalist. Con-

25. Darwall 1997, 306.
26. Nagel 1978, reprinted in Darwall et al. 1997, 325.
27. Korsgaard 1986, reprinted in Darwall et al. 1997, 375

sider preference-integrity first. Preference-integrity exists when an agent possesses a strong or decisive moral preference (e.g., honesty). Since preference-integrity is preference based and derives from utility theory, if the agent confronts two possible choices, *A* and *B*, *A* now reflects an act associated with the preference of honesty, whereas *B* is associated with the agent's other desires or preferences. In this case, the person of preference-integrity has reason to choose *A*. The key point of course is that for such an individual it was the strength of the moral preference of honesty and the pro-attitude toward the primacy of its satisfaction that provided the reason for choosing *A*, not any independent perceived rightness of the act. The compelling reason to act was a motivating reason based on the fulfillment of a preference; no link to a justifying reason exists or is necessary. Undoubtedly, there are many who think honesty is both good and also something they like, but it is the latter feature that constitutes the externalist reason for acting with preference-integrity. Therefore, since the externalist reason for acting honestly is the same as for any other act stemming from utility theory it is not a different kind of reason. The reason for acting on a decisive moral preference is the same as for any other preference.[28]

In contrast, persons of commitment-integrity need not make any reference to desires, preferences, or other interests in their reasons for action, except insofar as they are sufficient to overcome the will and prevent the internalist reason as being the decisive one. Consider again the agent faced with two possible choices, *A* and *B*. Choice *B* is still associated with the agent's preferences and desires. Choice *A*, however, is associated with the agent's judgment about what morality requires. The person of commitment-integrity has reflected on, consciously committed to, and identified with some moral principle such that *A* is seen as a moral duty. The person of commitment-integrity has internalist reason to choose *A* since it was the perceived truth of the moral principle that induced the agent to commit to and identify with it in the first place. The agent's other interests can come into play in a reason-defeating fashion. As suggested earlier, if the desire to choose *B* is sufficiently strong to overcome the agent's will to do what the agent judges to be right (*A*), the agent may choose *B*. In this case while the agent had internalist reason to choose *A*, the reason was not decisive or overriding. But failing to act on the internalist reason has a cost. The person of commitment-integrity has suffered some measure of incoherence (between principle and action), which inevitably destabilizes her identity or view of herself.

28. It might appear that utility theory offers a Humean internalist reason for acting. It does not because that kind of a reason requires justification as well as motivation. Standard utility theory does not require the agent to justify her own preferences, which are assumed to be exogenous.

3.3. An Assessment of Commitment-Integrity

The primary virtue of commitment-integrity is that it captures and incorporates the notions of volition, unity of character (coherence), and internalist decision making. Principles are chosen freely based upon their perceived truth and are applied consistently with motivations, other principles, and actions. Principles are generally context free, which ensures one kind of coherence. Unlike preference-integrity, a person of commitment-integrity is not free to lie to left-handed but not right-handed people. In addition, commitment-integrity does not suffer from the other weaknesses previously identified for preference-integrity. Commitment-integrity is *not* reductionist, self-referential, instrumental, or deterministic. Since commitment-integrity relies on principles and commitment it cannot be reductionist. Since it relies on internal reasons it cannot be self-referential or instrumental.[29] And since principles are chosen autonomously and applied by virtue of a free will, it cannot be deterministic.

It also turns out that commitment-integrity is compatible with an internalist psychological theory, cognitive moral development theory in psychology, and other theories focusing on the role of meaning in one's life. But, besides being difficult to work with, at least from the perspective of empirical researchers because of the severe information problems it poses, at least two classes of objections are possible. I will first address the objections, and then why one might fail to act with commitment-integrity.

Economists could lodge two kinds of complaints about the version of commitment-integrity discussed so far. First, they could deny the existence of moral principles, autonomous choice, and free will. To do so would be analogous, at least partly, to the debate about internalism versus externalism. Two points are worth considering. First, note that the decision-making model I have offered includes both internalist elements and also exogenous preferences. Thus, while it features moral principles, autonomy, and a free will, it also incorporates a standard characterization of preferences and their deterministic underpinnings. In fact, my characterization of strength of will is de-

29. If moral principles chosen are based on their perceived truth, coherence also requires that they be applied impartially. Under normal conditions, which will be discussed shortly, it is not coherent to lie to person *B* but not person *A*. Impartiality is a fundamental feature of moral principles and their application. It means that the decision maker must view herself, and her friends and loved ones, with equal standing to anyone else relevant to the situation. There is room for partiality in both morality and the account offered for preference-integrity, so there is room for the ethic of caring. It just does not seem possible to accommodate it in an account for commitment-integrity, at least as long as we require the principles chosen to be ones commonly recognized by moral philosophers. On related matters, see Blustein 1991.

pendent on the existence of standard preferences. Second, note that if we don't accept the kind of analysis offered here, then we are wed to descriptions of behavior where individuals are not autonomous, moral principles are just conceptual constructs with no behavioral implications, and a conception of a will that is not free. Of course those concepts are ubiquitous and used in everyday discourse, presumably because they have meaning. We act as if they have meaning. Moreover, their nonexistence would render moral responsibility meaningless because it would mean that individuals do not really *choose* their own acts, an implication few of us would seriously accept.

Economists might also complain about the need for a bias toward simplicity in the construction of theory. The argument might start that we already have a well-developed theory, utility theory, based on preferences and a few simple axioms and assumptions. It provides sufficient explanation for the types of behavior under consideration, especially if we carefully move from material to nonmaterial preferences, like those found in preference-integrity. If we have to consider integrity, the argument goes, preference-integrity is sufficient. In contrast, the information requirements for commitment-integrity are too burdensome because that conception further requires information about an individual's unobservable relationship to moral principles and strength of will. It is certainly true that the possibility of commitment-integrity would imply different, more costly empirical techniques than the ones economists typically use.[30] But such an argument defends reductionism in the name of methodological simplicity. Methodological simplicity is a worthy goal, but for the reasons given in the introduction, methodological realism is better. Just because a preference-based explanation *could* be used to explain certain behavior does not necessarily mean that it is the real explanation for the behavior.

At risk of overemphasizing the point, consider the conceptual analysis of the philosopher Thomas Nagel. He argues that the belief that all motivation stems from an agent's desire (preference) satisfaction rests on a mistake.[31] Al-

30. While difficult, the task is not impossible. As will be discussed in section 3.5, psychologists have been using the kind of interviewing techniques that would be required for some time.

31. Nagel 1978. John Searle is an example of another philosopher who takes reasons to be independent of desires, as demonstrated by the passage "in the case of human beings, it turns out that we have a rather large number of reasons that are not desires. These desire-independent reasons can form the ground for desires, but their being reasons for us does not depend on their being based on desires" (2001, 2). In his view, duties, obligations, and commitments all can be prior to and the cause of desire. Interestingly, and as an example of how confusing the internalism/externalism distinction can be, Nagel writes as an internalist, while Searle explicitly includes externalist considerations in his analysis, even though both focus their attention on desire-independent reasons.

though motivation to act might always require the presence of desire, that does not mean that desire underlies the motivation. Instead, the desire to act is motivated by a more primitive reason: the agent's conception of herself "as merely a person among others equally real." That she can put herself in another's place reveals that those interests are "someone's" interests, just as hers are. This recognition of another's reality thus provides both the reason (motivation) *and* the desire to act.

Another kind of objection to commitment-integrity might come from the proponents of multiple-utility or multiple-preference frameworks.[32] Multiple-utility models assume that individuals simultaneously possess different rankings of options, while multiple-preference models claim the existence of rankings over rankings. Both suffer from the same criticisms leveled against standard utility theory. Consider the more logically coherent case of the multiple-preference idea, which suggests that individuals possess higher-order preference rankings over their standard preference rankings. For instance, at the first-stage standard level, I may prefer lying and getting away with something over telling the truth and taking the consequences. However, my second-order preferences could be the opposite: I could prefer the ranking of "truth telling dominating lying" over the "lying dominating truth telling" one. In that case I might be heard to utter, "I want to lie but I wish I didn't want to." This state reveals an inner conflict that would be absent if I was instead able to align my first- and second-order preferences.

Harry Frankfurt would further claim that my choice is not based on free will because my first- and second-order desires are not in harmony. It seems unmistakably true that many people do care about the preferences they have and that multiple-preference models make progress in capturing that disposition. However, so long as higher-order preferences are truly preferences, and exogenously given ones at that, the analysis remains reductionist, self-referential, instrumental, and deterministic. It is reductionist because all dispositions are preferences or preference caused. It is self-referential and instrumental because it relies on desire-based reasons for motivation and action, even if it does include different externalist reasons that justify action at the second-order level. And Frankfurt's view notwithstanding, it is deterministic unless there is provision for the agent to act against *any* of the preferences attributed to her. I am aware of no framework that makes such allowances.

A final objection could target my handling of the will. It would appear

32. Philosopher Harry Frankfurt (1971) seems to be the primary source of the ideas, with other major contributors including Sen (1978) and Etzioni (1986). Also see Brennan 1989, Lutz 1993, and Brennan 1993 for a lively exchange on the merits of the idea. George 2001 offers a most recent explication and defense of the multiple-preference idea.

that the will only enters into the analysis insofar as its strength determines whether or not commitments can be followed. The model provides a precise metric for that determination. However, by itself that rendering would not seem adequate to capture the notion of a free will. Another aspect of the will is that which chooses among desires and principles. Kant explicitly distinguished between these two aspects of the will by introducing the concepts of *Wille* and *Willkur.*[33] The first refers to the choice of moral path, the second to the choice of actions. Note that my analysis also includes both aspects. Though it was not referred to as such, the *Wille* aspect of the will was included as that which chooses principles in the first place (or first stage). In my model, this aspect captures the "free" aspect of the will. Then the strength of will determines whether principle-based commitments can be actualized. That aspect captures the notion of *Willkur.*

3.4. Failures to Act with Commitment-Integrity

Later I will examine some factors that might enhance or promote integrity (see chapter 9, "On the Possibility of Integrity"), but here we can further elucidate the notion of commitment-integrity by examining why someone would not be a person of commitment-integrity. There are five reasons: (1) failure to choose moral principles, (2) weakness of will, (3) errors in judgment, (4) self-deception, and (5) moral exclusion. I will also discuss mutual deceit, which by itself does not compromise integrity, but when coupled with institutional failure can explain certain types of contractual failures, especially in business firms. Consider each reason in turn.

Two factors might influence why someone does not choose moral principles on which to base commitment-integrity. First, they may choose other principles instead. For instance, one could choose the principle of making their own preference satisfaction their highest concern. The principle of maximizing one's own welfare does not qualify for commitment-integrity primarily because the existence of moral principles is irrelevant for such a person. Such individuals are only concerned with their own preferences. If they possess qualifying preferences of sufficient intensity (e.g., honesty), they

33. See Beck 1960, 176–81. This reference is from White 2006, which also provides a model of moral decision making. He models free will as probabilistically choosing between moral duties and preferences, where the former are included in the agent's constraint. A weak will is one that chooses prudence over the moral path, which is judged superior by the agent. One difference between our models is that I treat moral principles as consciously chosen (rather than as constraints) and as the source of freedom. A probabilistic will could also be added without loss of generality.

might be characterized as persons of preference-integrity but not commitment-integrity.

Individuals might also choose to embrace other nonmoral principles. One could choose to commit to the principle that art is the highest good, and making art is the most important thing one could do. If a person had such a commitment, and they were also coherent as described earlier, they might be characterized by what Lynne McFall calls personal integrity. Personal integrity undoubtedly exists but is of limited relevance for the kinds of contexts considered in this book.

The other factor in why one might not embrace moral principles as her own is that she has not considered the possibility, or, if she did, dismissed it. For such people, preference satisfaction is likely to be the default position. The entire issue of moral motivation is considered in the next section.

The second reason a person might not be characterized by commitment-integrity is because they have a sufficiently weak will. Philosophers call the condition of weak will *akrasia.* Earlier we put some flesh on what constitutes the term *weak,* that is, the will to act is less than the utility difference between the fulfillment of some competing desire and the desire to act in accordance with commitment. In this case, the person has consciously chosen principles to commit to and identify with, but lacks sufficient power to overcome their competing desires. They may well intend to act on their principles but are otherwise unable to do so. Since intent cannot be the criterion, the issue turns on coherence. As we now know, someone who cannot meet the coherence condition between principle and act cannot be characterized as a person of commitment-integrity. Weakness of will provides one reason for incoherence.

Errors in judgment constitute another reason for incoherence. The question is, could persons of commitment-integrity make sincere mistakes in applying chosen moral principles and yet remain persons of commitment-integrity? Again, intent is not the issue. In many contexts it seems unlikely that errors in judgment would be a problem. Most real-life cases of truth-telling versus lying are clear-cut. But complex cases require more information and higher levels of cognition, which increases the probability of mistakes. Cognitive limitations and the cost of deliberation mean that we are boundedly rational.[34] Moreover, when principles conflict, mistakes can be made. Coherence also demands consistency in the chosen principles themselves. One who misjudges two principles to be consistent suffers from incoherence and thus cannot be said to be acting with integrity.

Intentional deception is just a case of opportunistic self-interest, an ad-

34. Conlisk 1996.

mittedly important one that will be returned to later, but nevertheless one that does not constitute a separate reason for failure to act with commitment-integrity.

On the other hand, the case of self-deception is complex. The claim would be that the person chose principles she committed to and identified with, had sufficient will to overcome competing desires, but instead deceived herself into believing that acting according to desire was what the relevant principle actually called for. Thus the failure to act out of commitment-integrity originated from a deception perpetrated against herself. The problem with that explanation as an independent cause is, as Bandura writes, "It is logically impossible to deceive oneself into believing something, while simultaneously knowing it to be false."[35] One cannot *think* something to be true while *knowing* it to be false; one cannot think something to be false while knowing it to be true. For some, no amount of fiddling with the concept will fix this contradiction. Others are more permissive, treating self-deception as a sort of self-delusion or by treating it analogously with an interpersonal deception.[36] Many people do seem to compartmentalize their experiences. Whatever its conceptual shortcomings, self-deception is commonly used to describe people who somehow fool themselves and/or people who do not seek information in order to keep themselves intentionally uninformed. Otherwise, what might be first thought of as self-deception may instead refer to a weak will if the agent really does know what is true and required, but is unable to actualize it in the face of competing desires.

A final reason why someone may not be a person of integrity is if they engage in moral exclusion, as Susan Opotow notes.

> Moral exclusion occurs when individuals or groups are perceived as outside the boundary in which moral values, rules, and considerations of fairness apply. Those who are morally excluded are perceived as nonentities, expendable, or undeserving. Consequently, harming or exploiting them appears to be appropriate, acceptable, or just.[37]

Moral exclusion seems to result from psychological distance, or unconnectedness. Since all but the enlightened tend to differentiate their external experiences, people create categories and boundaries in order to organize their in-

35. Bandura 1991, 94.
36. Taylor (1971) treats self-deception as one of the most important cases of failure of integrity without addressing the apparent contradiction. Blustein (1991, 106–8) discusses the contradiction and attempted strategies to overcome it.
37. Opotow 1990, 1.

ternal experience. Any individuals or group with whom a person feels a certain affinity may then be included within that person's moral boundaries. But if that affinity is not present, then the possibility (if not necessity) of moral exclusion exists.

Of course moral exclusion has been responsible for some of history's greatest atrocities. Slavery has always been rationalized by exempting some from the same moral standards that apply to others. Much of the killing in war, and seemingly all of the killing in genocides, have been rationalized by conceiving victims as lesser humans. These kinds of mass atrocities require institutional rationalizations—justifications concealing true interests—perpetrated by states or by religious, social, or cultural groups. But because moral principles are by their very nature universal, one could not selectively embrace these kinds of social rationalizations and still be considered a person of moral integrity. It does not matter if one happens to feel close to a victim or not.

Social exclusion also occurs in milder forms. In contexts that are the subject of this book, for instance, one may disregard the moral standing of another because of some real or perceived infraction that causes harm. Lying to a liar represents the quintessential case. From a normative moral perspective, lying could only be permitted if it prevents great harm. So lying to a liar is generally not the appropriate action, especially if alternatives exist.[38] Moreover, the empirical evidence suggests that people are sensitive to the harm caused by their lies and are more likely to lie when the harm is judged to be low.[39] Uri Gneezy suggests that is why people are more accepting of lies and fraud against large organizations than against individuals who are more likely to be disproportionately harmed.[40] And many people do reciprocate both "nice" behaviors and "mean" behaviors. Reciprocation underlies the notion of fairness, recently most popular with economists, and will be discussed in chapters 4 and 6.

Unlike the five reasons just considered, one could be considered a person of commitment-integrity and still engage in mutual deceit. Mutual deceit pertains to those persons who have chosen truth telling (not lying) as their principle, so coherence requires that such people do not then engage in acts of lying. I will discuss lying more fully in chapter 5, but are there contexts where it *is* acceptable to lie? According to Sissela Bok, the issue hinges on whether each of the agents knows the rules of the game and accepts those rules.[41]

38. Bok 1978. This topic will be extensively discussed in chapters 5 and 6.
39. Gneezy 2005; DePaulo et al. 1996.
40. Gneezy 2005, 391.41. Bok 1978.
41. Bok 1978.

People lie wildly in games of poker, but that does not mean that they cannot be persons of commitment-integrity. By themselves these kinds of lies are not a problem because each of the participants expects and accepts such behavior. The same could be said for some buyer-seller situations and interactions between spouses. I expect the car dealer to misrepresent their lowest price and I almost appreciate my wife telling me I look good even as my body rebels with age. These kinds of white lies are a form of deceit, but a special kind where the parties are complicit. However, if an agent (rationally) views certain interactions as if they are governed by mutual deceit, perhaps because of some institutional flaw, then some productive trades might not occur. For instance, if some workplace lacks clear, fair employment agreements, then even workers of integrity might promise to work hard but not honor that promise because they view the workplace as one characterized by mutual deceit. The solution in that case is not additional monitoring by the firm, but rather instituting clear, fair agreements that workers see as morally binding on their promises. That topic will be investigated in detail in chapter 6.

3.5. Psychological Foundations

The previous sections tried to carefully lay out the conceptual foundations of commitment-integrity, in some cases by distinguishing it from preference-integrity. That required a fair amount of philosophical analysis. This section does the same thing for the psychological foundations by appealing to different views of cognition.

Finding the psychological foundations for utility theory, and by extension preference-integrity, is not difficult. According to the careful, if somewhat idiosyncratic, accounts of Augusto Blasi and Thomas Wren, the majority of psychologists over much of the twentieth century explained moral action the same way they do any other action, that is, with incentives and reinforcement.[42] With some important exceptions, economics and psychological orthodoxy converge on this point.

Blasi's concern is with the link between moral belief and moral action, the traditional domain of empirical psychology. He suggests that the orthodoxy in learning theories, ethnology, some psychoanalysis, and much social psychology could agree on four general propositions. To paraphrase, the first says that people possess action tendencies like habits and traits leading to different behaviors that, depending on the relevant culture, may be labeled

42. Blasi 1983; Wren 1991.

"moral." Second, the final action performed depends on the interplay among the tendencies themselves and the relevant situation, and in principle could be precisely predicted by knowing these antecedent factors. Third, cognitive processes facilitate connections between tendencies, situations, and actions. Fourth, cognitive processes do not provide moral reasons in the sense that they motivate action. Rather, to the extent moral reasons exist they provide rationalizations or a self-protecting account of actions already performed. For the orthodoxy, Blasi contends, cognition refers mainly to images, memories, verbal labels, and acts to facilitate associations. That account fits utility theory and preference-integrity well because preferences can be thought of as the relevant tendencies, with cognition facilitating rationality. The rational economic agent acts on his own preferences after (cognitively) evaluating the ones most relevant to the situation at hand.

There is a different notion of cognition. Blasi contrasts the preceding version with that of cognitive developmentalists. For the latter, "cognition refers to understanding, construction of meanings, and coherent logical structures, and functions mainly to provide moral meanings to otherwise neutral actions."[43] For cognitive developmentalists, cognition defines actions as morally relevant and then provides the motivation to act. Blasi contends that it is this different use of the meaning of the word *cognition* that makes it difficult for the different schools of thought to understand one another.

Thomas Wren pursues this line of reasoning further by assessing the so-called cognitive revolution in psychology. He argues that most psychologists fall in Blasi's first camp of cognitivists, which further means that they provide externalist reasons for moral action. For philosophers, externalism means that justifying reasons are independent from motivating reasons. So it is for Wren's classification of the first seven kinds of psychologies, from the least to most cognitive, which starts with Skinner's radical behavioralism and goes up to "self-control in the delay of gratification" theories. Perhaps most pertinent for preference-integrity (and utility theory in general) is number four on the list, "approach-avoidance" theory. In this theory individuals are "caught in an inherently non-rational force-field of desires."[44] Desires conflict, and the strongest one wins (motivates action)—just like in utility maximization. Again, there is no role for the individual either to assess the truth of moral propositions or to in some way rank her own desires by any means other than intensity. The individual's cognitive ability permits her to know her interests

43. Blasi 1983, 181. My colleague in psychology, John Ricards, contends that all cognitive psychologists hold this more expansive view.

44. Wren 1991, 51.

given the context. Once again, the focus on desire as being the source of motivation squares nicely with utility theory and preference-integrity, so long as honesty is the dominant desire.

The primary criticism of this approach, and it's an important one, is that it endows individuals with severely limited cognitive powers and makes self-interested actions based on desires the *sole* force capable of motivating action.[45] While desire-based reasons for action are undeniably powerful, the empirical evidence casts strong doubt on that being the only source of motivation.

Now consider the psychological foundation for commitment-integrity, which is a bit less obvious. That foundation hinges on the second notion of cognition, that is, the one that links moral reasoning and moral motivations. The discussion proceeds, then, with a review of two more theories, one well-known, one not: first the cognitive development psychology of Piaget and Kohlberg, then the philosophically inspired personal project analysis found in social psychology. According to these theories, instead of individuals maximizing their own welfare, the objective is to achieve psychological equilibrium, which ultimately requires consistency between what one believes to be true and how one acts. Equilibrium, then, is intimately tied to the concept of coherence that underlies commitment-integrity. It also turns out that it can give people a sense of meaning in their lives.

Cognitive Development Theories: Piaget and Kohlberg

According to Wren, cognitive development theories start from the stronger view of cognition, one that refers to understanding and enables moral meanings. They share three other themes: (1) development proceeds through stages, (2) development stages are structural, and (3) the defining process is "interiorization." Piaget thought moral development occurred in two distinct stages, Kohlberg six. Both Piaget and Kohlberg thought that individuals seek cognitive equilibrium, or the logical stability associated with better thinking.

According to Piaget, equilibrium occurs when individuals are able to receive an incoming stimulus, perhaps by modifying the stimulus itself, without having to modify their current thought structure. This process is known as assimilation. If, however, assimilation is not possible because the incoming

45. This kind of limited cognition is not the same as bounded rationality. The latter results from limitations on information processing and the cost of deliberation (Conlisk 1996). That is quite different from saying that individuals are not even permitted to evaluate their own preferences, reasons, or the truth of propositions.

stimulus cannot be accommodated by the current thought structure, the thought structure itself changes. This process is called accommodation.[46] Thus, not only do individuals seek cognitive equilibrium within stages, it is also the driving force as individuals progress through ascending stages. Structuralism refers to "general organizing principles or patterns of thought rather than specific moral beliefs or opinions."[47] The idea is that ascending stages of development refer to higher levels of thinking rather than to specific thoughts or contents. Interiorization is a process by which "concrete actions are transformed into verbalized moral judgments."[48] To further clarify the ideas, consider both of the theory's main proponents in turn.

Piaget assumed that individuals are ultimately motivated by the search for truth and the desire to understand reality. He held the issue of morality versus nonmorality to be a matter of adequate versus inadequate knowledge, as in Plato's rationalistic view.[49] So, perfect morality could be achieved when one achieved perfect knowledge, where knowledge itself depends on cognitive development. At any given level of cognitive development, the structure of thought crucially depends on actions because actions convey information about reality, and also because actions precede and then are transformed into mental representations (interiorization). Since actions provide information about reality, which the individual cares to know about, the individual tends toward cognitive equilibrium by increasingly aligning her understanding of reality with that information. This process squares nicely with the informational roles assigned to society and culture in the earlier discussion describing how individuals consciously reflect. Piaget took interiorizations to be true articulations of reality rather than self-defensive rationalizations.

Following Kant, Piaget distinguished between two separate stages of moral development: heteronomy, then autonomy. In the first, the individual defers to external authority. In the second there is self-determination based on mutual respect for one's peers.[50] Individuals develop and move from the lower to higher stage by the process described here, that is, by assimilating and accommodating information to understanding. If there is some kind of inconsistency between the information conveyed in current actions and the current cognitive structure, the tendency toward cognitive equilibrium assures that the result will be increased understanding. Morally inconsistent be-

46. Boden 1980, 7.
47. Colby and Kohlberg 1987, 2.
48. Wren 1991, 111.
49. Blasi 1983.
50. Wren 1991.

havior could only occur from either compulsion or akrasia.[51] Irrationality could only stem from imperfect knowledge. Piaget's empirical work with children led him to believe that a child's moral judgments were linked to the quality of her social interactions, but also that it wasn't particularly difficult or unusual for an adult to reach stage 2 thinking.

To see how cognitive development can provide the psychological basis for commitment-integrity, it will be instructive to further investigate the work of Piaget's torchbearer, Lawrence Kohlberg. From the late 1950s to the late 1980s, Kohlberg engaged in a research project rooted in Piaget's work, but one that ultimately became paradigmatic in its own right. Among the big differences between them is that Kohlberg identified three levels with two stages each of cognitive moral development. He also helped to introduce the "standard issue moral judgment interview and scoring system," a standardized interview technique that seeks to reliably measure cognitive moral development. The technique has been used by many different researchers in many different cultural contexts to assess individuals' cognitive moral development. The following offers a brief sketch of Kohlberg's theory.

Kohlberg identifies three foundational assumptions underlying his cognitive moral development theory: (1) phenomenalism, (2) structuralism, and (3) constructivism.[52] In moral psychology, the first assumption means that moral judgments reflect rational thought rather than unconscious motives. These judgments must be assessed from the agent's own perspective, and it is further assumed that moral judgments are important determinants of actual conduct. The second, structuralism, is a view that the particular content of thought can be differentiated from the structure of thought. *Structure* refers to "general organizing principles or patterns of thought," which is the level researchers try to measure with Kohlberg's interview techniques. *Constructivism* means that individuals construct meaning for themselves. This meaning, in turn, is dependent upon the individual's level of cognitive development. As the individual develops, she enters new stages representing different ways of thinking that are more and more complex. Since each new stage becomes possible only after reaching understanding at the preceding stage, stage development occurs in a predictable sequence. For any given problem, individuals use the highest stage of cognitive moral development available to them.[53]

---

51. Blasi 1983, 189.
52. Colby and Kohlberg 1987, vol. 1, chapter 1.
53. Wren (1991, 117) also notes that Kohlberg's notion of interiorization was more complex than Piaget's in that moral judgments could also guide new behaviors (as opposed to just the other way around).

Expanding on those assumptions, Kohlberg and his colleagues identify three levels of development with two stages each. The first level is called *preconditional:* stage 1 is characterized by "heteronomous" morality; stage 2 by individualism, instrumental purpose, and exchange. At the preconditional level individuals take the "concrete individual" perspective in which one's own interests are central, and rules are viewed as external to oneself. Stage 1 thinkers seek to avoid punishment, stage 2 to meet one's own needs. Based on the evidence, Kohlberg estimates that the preconditional level characterizes "most children under 9, some adolescents, and many adolescent and adult criminal offenders."[54] While to my knowledge not mentioned by Kohlberg, preconditional-level thinking is also the type of thinking supposed by economists for *homo economicus.* He could have referenced from any standard microeconomics text when he wrote, "Since each person's primary aim is to pursue his or her own interests, the perspective of at Stage 2 is pragmatic: to maximize satisfaction of one's own needs and desires while minimizing negative consequences to the self."[55]

The second level is called *conventional:* stage 3 is characterized by mutual interpersonal expectations, relationships, and interpersonal conformity, while stage 4 is characterized by "social system, and conscience." At this second level, individuals take a "member of society" perspective. They identify with the rules and expectations of others, and derive their morality from social norms. Stage 3 thinkers seek to be good persons in both their own and others' eyes, perhaps appealing to the Golden Rule. Stage 4 thinkers source their morality in divine or natural law and point to the importance of social duties as a way of maintaining social harmony. Kohlberg estimates that most adolescents and adults in most societies fall into this conventional level of thinking. With its reliance on socially shared norms, in one way this level might also characterize the way sociologists think about why people behave the way they do. In another way it does not, because cognitive moral thinking presupposes that individuals rationally choose which reasons to act upon. Most sociological positions do not attribute such autonomy to individual decision makers.

The third level is called *postconventional:* stage 5 is characterized by social contract and individual rights, while stage 6 is characterized by universal ethical principles. Significantly, stage 5 is called the "human rights and social welfare morality" stage, to signify that individuals at this stage recognize universal values and rights as the key to a moral society. Moreover, meeting

54. Colby and Kohlberg 1987, 16.
55. Colby and Kohlberg 1987, 26.

obligations derives from mutual respect of persons. At this third level, individuals take the "prior-to-society" perspective. Individuals at this level understand general moral principles and can apply them. Legal and social laws should conform with general moral principles, but in the event that they conflict the individual may be compelled to choose in favor of the latter. Kohlberg estimates that only the minority of adults reach this postconventional level. Of course philosophers argue that normative ethics requires thinking of this sort.[56]

To form estimates of the proportion of people characterized by each level, Kohlberg relies on the evidence from the interview technique he developed with Anne Colby, called "the standard issue moral judgment interview and scoring system." Subjects are first confronted with a moral dilemma by an interviewer and then queried about how to respond and why. For instance, a man (Heinz) has a wife who is dying of a certain type of cancer, for which a local druggist has an expensive, experimental cure, but the druggist will not discount the drug so that Heinz can afford to buy it. Should Heinz steal the drug? The interviewer classifies the subject's responses according to an elaborate scoring system, which takes into account certain "modal" and "value" elements, as well as norms. Modal elements refer to reasons to uphold (or not) the normative order, while value elements refer to the types of consequences with which the subject may be concerned (e.g., egoistic, utilitarian, harmony-serving, or fairness). The interviewer looks for whatever norms the subject may offer, which are not predetermined, as a clue to why the subject thinks one course of action dominates another. The scoring system is then used to assign subjects to the relevant stage.[57]

---

56. Wren (1991) views Kohlberg's theory as based on internal reasons and argues that sometimes Kohlberg's ascending stages are mistakenly interpreted as a movement from a sort of externalism to an internalism. For instance, it may appear that individuals unreflectively act on (narrow) self-interest in stages 1 and 2, and social norms in stages 3 and maybe 4, and only really start to consider the perceived truth of moral propositions on their actions in stages 5 and 6. Sometimes Kohlberg himself contributed to this misunderstanding with imprecise language. But on Wren's reading all stages are internalist in that individuals rationally consider the moral systems available to them prior to a prospective decision. The difference lies more in the source of the moral system. So, for instance, a child at stage 1 makes all moral judgments based on physical properties and consequences. For such a child the moral system is straightforward: something is wrong if it brings bad consequences to the self, good if the consequences are good. At higher stages the rightness of an act is determined more by its perceived conformity with social norms. For Kohlberg, even children are endowed with the ability for rational deliberation, and that is what separates his theory from those based more on reinforcement and/or unreflective responses.

57. As one example, the response "Heinz should steal the drug because his wife needs it or will die without it" represents stage 2 thinking because it is instrumental, refers only to the woman's physical needs, focuses on supporting life as the chosen issue, and neglects any higher-stage idea about the value of life (Colby and Kohlberg 1987, 46). In contrast, the response "Heinz should steal the

At its peak, Kohlberg's theory was among the most cited in the behavioral sciences.[58] By using the interview technique mentioned here, or some close variant, overwhelming evidence indicates that the theory's main predictions are supported. For instance, after analyzing forty-five studies of moral development in twenty-seven different countries, John Snarey concludes that people do move through stages (especially the first four) just as Kohlberg theorized, and that stage skipping and stage regression are rare.[59] Moral judgment tends to advance with time and formal education. Snarey could not find any appreciable evidence that Kohlberg's interview technique is culturally biased, especially when it is suitably adapted. He did suggest, however, that a richer theory might include collective solidarity, a value sometimes found in traditional folk cultures and working-class communities. Others have criticized Kohlberg's theory for being gender biased because it relies on notions of justice rather than values like caring.[60] Nevertheless, the evidence does not support the notion that there are sex differences in moral development.[61] While there could still be an important role for caring or emotions in normative moral theory or actual moral deliberations, it is fairly clear that moral judgment has a predictable, universal, and cognitive dimension.[62]

A more problematic concern might target the link between moral judgment and moral behavior. In his early work, Kohlberg *assumed* a positive, significant link. The sensible, intuitive idea is that our actions are influenced

---

drug because the right to life supersedes or transcends the right to property" is an example of stage 5 reasoning. Here, the norm once again is life-preserving, but the focal element is to serve human dignity and autonomy (60). It should be emphasized that interviewers do not base their scoring on just these short answers but rather on a series of probing follow-up questions (e.g., what if the sick person is not Heinz's wife?).

58. Endler, Rushton, and Roediger 1978.

59. Snarey 1985. Also see Colby and Kohlberg 1987; Kohlberg 1984. The latter in particular provides a good summary of Kohlberg's critics and Kohlberg's responses.

60. See, for instance, Gilligan 1982. Similarly, Kohlberg has been accused of being too "Kantian." Puka (1991) persuasively argues that while the charge has some basis, Kohlberg's theoretical analysis survives the relaxation of some of the more restrictive Kantian assumptions and that, most important, the empirical analysis of stage scoring does not make the same assumptions in the first place.

61. Summarizing his review and meta-analysis, Lawrence Walker writes, "Of the 108 samples summarized . . . , only eight clearly indicated significant differences favoring males. Furthermore, several of these studies yielding sex differences favoring men were methodologically flawed, primarily because sex and occupational/educational differences were confounded. In addition, most studies reporting sex differences relied on early stage definitions and scoring procedures" (1984, 688). Also see Walker 1991.

62. James Rest, one of Kohlberg's students, modified Kohlberg's approach slightly in order to improve its accuracy. Rest's questionnaire, the "Defining Issues Test," became immensely popular in its own right. After 500 studies using this approach from 20 different countries, Rest (1986, 176–79) concludes that the evidence further supports claims like the ones just mentioned.

by our thoughts. If one thinks a moral judgment to be true, one might act accordingly. Of course other thoughts and "mediating" factors could short-circuit the connection, so it is important to look at the evidence. The seminal article remains Augusto Blasi's 1980 review of seventy-five studies. He found that in fifty-seven of those studies, a positive significant relationship between moral judgment and behavior existed, but also that the strength of the relationship was modest because correlation coefficients were typically around .3.[63] While this modest relationship might be a cause for concern, it should be noted that it is necessary neither for Kohlberg's thesis nor for the one in this book that moral reasoning causes action, especially on a one-to-one basis. As mentioned when discussing Piaget earlier, inconsistencies could occur from either compulsion or an insufficiently strong will. Kohlberg himself addressed the issue in his later writings by suggesting that both responsibility and also strength of will need to be included when determining how a person actually behaves.[64] Earlier in this chapter I added self-deception and moral exclusion to the list. In any case, it is both possible and expected that such mediating factors would influence actions, and that is a topic that will be revisited again and again throughout this book.[65]

Personal Project Analysis

Personal project analysis provides a psychological justification for commitment-integrity from a slightly different angle.[66] Personal projects are consciously chosen acts, either current or planned. Making a lot of money and telling the truth are two examples. Typically, psychologists assume that well-

63. The story is similar for Rest's DIM approach. See Rest 1986, 134–35.

64. Kohlberg 1984, chapter 7.

65. Consider a sampling of other cognitive theorists. Hoffman (1991), in the spirit of Hume, bases his theory of moral motivation on the capacity for empathy. Cognition facilitates empathetic action because it enables situational sensitivity and judgments about consequences. His account appears to be most consistent with preference-integrity. Bandura's (1991) account of moral behavior includes cognition in the manner of Piaget and Kohlberg, but also social or environmental factors and internal sanctions as well. Each determinant affects the others bidirectionally. Moral behavior is most likely to occur when to act otherwise would not be easily self-excusable and when the reactions of important peers would be compatible. Bandura's account is something of a hybrid and is thus difficult to place as possibly underlying (only) either preference- or commitment-integrity. Blasi's (1983) theory is squarely in the Piaget-Kohlberg tradition but adds the notion of the self as a way to correct some perceived weaknesses. One's self-definition influences judgments about one's responsibilities. While there will be competing needs, one's responsibilities are then actualized by a tendency toward self-consistency. Blasi (206) in fact defines integrity as being "a responsible actualization of what one knows to be right and true." For this reason his account is fully compatible with the one for commitment-integrity offered here.

66. Little 1983; McGregor and Little 1998.

being derives solely from happiness. In referring to personal projects, happiness, in turn, is said to derive from efficacy, or the likelihood of one's projects being successful. Personal project analysis theorizes that in addition to happiness, well-being has another source, namely, meaning. Meaning, in turn, depends on integrity, or the degree of consistency between one's projects and one's self or identity. Meaning is associated with feelings of purpose, connectedness, and growth. This second source of well-being is emphasized in the wisdom traditions of numerous religions and philosophies.

Personal project analysis, then, predicts that personal projects can serve two separable functions. First, they can instrumentally promote efficacy and happiness. Second, they can symbolically represent core aspects (i.e., values and commitments) of the self, such as integrity, to promote meaning. McGregor and Little (1998) report results from two experimental studies using college students to support their hypotheses. In particular, their findings suggest that well-being has the two separate dimensions as described, and that "participants whose personal projects were consistent with core elements of their self-identity reported higher levels of meaning than did those whose projects were less reflective of self-identity" (505).

The authors opine that although efficacy might sometimes serve as a surrogate for integrity, a good well-being strategy would balance both considerations. Sole reliance on achieving consonance between one's core aspects of the self and one's personal projects may yield great meaning, but at the cost of a state of unhappiness or dissatisfaction. In contrast, the sole pursuit of "doing well" may lead to disconnection and meaninglessness. The authors report literature that shows that a preoccupation with success is associated with poorer mental health and that those surrounded by success tend to feel disconnected and lacking in meaningful contacts. But contemporary forces appear to tempt us to favor efficacy-following strategies over integrity ones. First, the cultural norm of the American dream is at its very heart efficacy-based. Second, it feels good to be happy, at least in the short run and until habituation sets in. And finally, in order to act with integrity one has to deliberate how to act in accordance with one's identity. Research shows that such self-focus on one's own behavior decreases well-being in the short run. It is for these reasons and others that we need to be reminded of the importance of integrity.[67]

67. Interestingly, economists' recent work on the "economics of happiness" can further contribute to this area. Based on both subjective satisfaction data and objective data (e.g., suicide rates), Oswald (1997) concludes that the economic growth experienced by industrialized Western societies has increased happiness only marginally, at best. Frank (1997b) suggests that the reason people support growth even if it will not increase average happiness is because individual happiness, here

To summarize, this section provides the psychological underpinnings for both preference-integrity and commitment-integrity. The orthodoxy supports preference-integrity if honesty is a dominant desire. Desire provides the motive, which is made relevant to given situations by cognitive processes that enable context-dependent associations. Even personal project analysis supports preference-integrity for those who choose honesty as projects to instrumentally fulfill. Commitment-integrity is solidly based on cognitive moral development, and also personal project analysis. The cognitive moral development literature sources an individual's motive to the search for truth and cognitive equilibrium. As in the account for commitment-integrity detailed earlier in this chapter, individuals must reason for themselves about which principles to act upon. The notion of cognition is expanded to include understanding, which in turn links moral reasons and moral acts. Most fundamentally, though, the notion of cognitive equilibrium provides the psychological basis for coherence in commitment-integrity. Coherence is a normative requirement of commitment-integrity, and cognitive equilibrium is the reason one would choose coherence. But even if one believes a moral principle to be true and is committed to it, that does not mean that the reason to act will be decisive. Compulsion and/or akrasia could mediate between moral reasoning and final act. Personal project analysis also provides a psychological foundation for commitment-integrity because it identifies meaning as an important source of well-being, and symbolically aligning one's projects with one's chosen identity confers meaning.

3.6. Conclusion

I have offered an account of two different kinds of integrity. The first, preference-integrity, exists when an individual has a strong and decisive preference for honesty. Preference-integrity fits easily into the usual machinery of utility theory. The second, commitment-integrity, exists when an individual first chooses moral principles to commit to and identify with, then acts in accordance with those commitments. The latter account includes the notions of conscious reflection, the will, and coherence. It is also consistent with the way

meaning efficacy, is based on how one views one's own material standing relative to others. Each individual strives to obtain more than her peers. But even if this strategy really was the key to happiness, it is doomed to failure because if each uses this strategy happiness can only persist until others catch up. Other approaches seek to find objective contributors to well-being, like various freedoms, in order to actualize individual autonomy. For a brief review and comparison to subjective well-being ideas, see Comin 2005.

philosophers think about integrity. A philosophical assessment and psychological foundations were offered for both kinds of integrity.

A natural question one might ask is why we need two kinds of integrity. For some it will already be difficult enough to accept the inclusion of honesty as a preference in the utility function, so why go further and bother with commitments, the will, and the like? There are two answers to that question. First, as I have discussed at length, preference-integrity suffers from some significant methodological weaknesses that are not pertinent to commitment-integrity. Methodological realism suggests an understanding of both accounts.

The second answer has to do with the different implications associated with each type of integrity. Someone who has an overriding preference for honesty will act similarly to one who is committed to honesty in similar contexts. But for those endowed with a weaker preference or for those whose preferences change easily, the similarity may end. In particular, anything that changes a person's preference for honesty or changes the costs and benefits of behaving honestly could change the behavior of an individual (previously) described as exhibiting preference-integrity. Since we usually assume that preferences are not within an individual's control, to the extent they are malleable, the foundation of preference-integrity is shaky.

Commitment-integrity is only indirectly affected by changes in preferences (or the costs and benefits of preferences), that is, only insofar as it changes the utility difference between acting according to one's commitments or not. If that difference changes the comparison to the will, behavior could change as a result of the preference change, if only through an indirect route. But a person with a sufficiently strong will continues to act in accordance with their commitments even in the face of preference changes.

The reverse is also true. Something that changes one's commitments will change the behavior of one with commitment integrity but not preference-integrity. As we will see in chapter 9, the evidence suggests that moral training and moral leadership can affect behavior. For cognitive moral development psychologists like Lawrence Kohlberg, the link between moral education and moral behavior occurs because of increased moral reasoning. Since moral reasoning is different from moral preferences, anything that changes the former can change behavior independently of the latter.

Finally, I would like to return to the question of methodology. I have sketched how commitment-integrity could be theoretically modeled. The question remains as to how it could be empirically tested. A virtue of utility theory is that it starts with some simple assumptions on preferences (and a few others) and generates testable implications for which ample methodological machinery exists. Typically, we can find data on choices and relevant economic variables (i.e., prices, incomes, incentives), which can then be analyzed with econometric techniques to see if posited relationships exist. Even then, in many cases observed choices are a poor indicator of true preferences. Timur Kuran's work on preference falsification shows that sometimes people conform with social preferences and conceal their private preferences, perhaps out of fear or in order to enhance their reputations. For instance, preference falsification could explain why the major polls incorrectly (and spectacularly) failed to pick the winner of the 1990 Nicaraguan presidential election.[68]

The possibility of commitment-integrity makes the task even more difficult. In particular, the possibility of commitments and wills of varying strengths implies that preference relations cannot be inferred from observed choices and relevant economic variables for reasons beyond even preference falsification. Now the task is not just to distinguish private from social preferences, but also to disentangle any preferences from commitments to principles. While modern survey techniques can sometimes get at deep-seated attitudes by reducing the probability of social desirability bias, different kinds of research techniques will be required to access individuals' commitments and strength of will.[69] We will need to use interview techniques based on moral dilemmas, like the ones inspired by Lawrence Kohlberg and more recently used by neuroscientists. Interview techniques of this sort are costly and relatively unfamiliar for some social scientists, but to continue to ignore them risks omitting important variables in behavioral analyses.

Now that the foundations of preference-integrity and commitment-integrity have been established in some detail, it will be instructive to see how a person of each type might behave in social situations. The first one to consider is a stylized social dilemma, a topic most often studied with game theory.

---

68. Kuran 1995, 340. Interestingly, prior to the election an experiment indicated these polls were unreliable. When interviewers polled respondents, three different kinds of pens were used to record responses: one with a logo for each of the two favored parties and one neutrally colored. The logo pens clearly influenced the responses, while the neutral pen respondents disproportionately said they were going to vote for the loser. While the experiment did not predict the winner, it did suggest the possibility of preference falsification.

69. For instance, researchers can ask questions about how a protagonist might view a situation rather than about the respondent's own view, in order to reduce social desirability bias. For a good reference on how surveyors elicit truthful responses, see Tourangeau, Lips, and Rasinski 2000.

Chapter 4

Social Dilemmas and Game Theory

Game theory is the study of interdependent decision making. It analyzes situations in which outcomes depend on the decisions of more than one individual. Social dilemmas are a particular type of game in which the individual's self-interest conflicts with the optimal social outcome. For instance, self-interested individuals optimize by not paying for public goods like public radio or television but consume them anyway. However, if everyone did the same presumably everyone would be worse off because the services would not be provided. Properly constructed, it is always instrumentally rational to withhold contributions. If others provide the service the agent consumes without paying for it; if the service isn't provided the agent is no worse off because she didn't contribute. More broadly, it is in my interest that you but not I contribute to all that makes society civilized (taxes to pay for protection, public health, education, social safety nets, etc.).

Or consider the overanalyzed Prisoner's Dilemma game, the focal point of this chapter. Two suspects in a crime are caught. The district attorney has enough evidence to put the suspects in jail, but a confession would increase jail time. So the DA tells each suspect that if one confesses but the other does not, the confessor gets a light sentence while the other gets a lengthy stay in jail. If neither confesses, each gets some jail time, but less than if both confess. It turns out that while both would be better off keeping their mouths shut, instrumental rationality dictates that both sing like birds.

The Prisoner's Dilemma game describes a lot of two-agent interactions, especially the kind where agents might misrepresent their intended actions (e.g., a prospective employer says she will provide a good working environment when it is cheaper for her not to, and the prospective employee says she will work hard even though she really likes to drink lots of coffee). Yet we know that people *do* contribute to public goods, pay their taxes, vote, leave tips, help strangers, keep their agreements, and cooperate in all manner of experimental games in contraposition to their interests as usually concocted. The question is why, and what role could integrity play?

To make the discussion more concrete, I will introduce the Prisoner's Dilemma game with a numerical example. This makes it easier to both properly understand the social dilemma and also see the various explanations for how cooperation could result. We will also see that the notion of preference-integrity yields novel results for contexts where nonbinding agreements are made. Those with sufficient preference-integrity might keep their word with partners of unknown intent, contrary to traditional predictions.

The second part of the chapter considers the more recent development of evolutionary game theory. Evolutionary biology, metaphorically or literally, provides the inspiration for a new sort of game theory in which the focus becomes traits (e.g., preferences) and how they are selected for over time. An evolutionarily stable equilibrium is a state of affairs in which existing traits get the same payoffs, and no other traits could invade and get a higher payoff. These kinds of analyses can reveal the evolutionary conditions in which cooperation and selfishness exist simultaneously and persist over time. We will see that preference-integrity can fit into at least some kinds of evolutionary analyses, but that commitment-integrity could not because of its nonnatural ethical foundations (the individual makes judgments about right versus wrong in committing to moral principles). Still, persons of commitment-integrity could be affected by evolutionary forces to the extent that anything that affects preferences could change the cost of commitments relative to a given will, thereby indirectly affecting acts chosen. Thus, while commitment-integrity can not be naturalized, it could include naturalistic elements and hence constitute a framework that accommodates both.

4.1. The Prisoner's Dilemma

Consider the Prisoner's Dilemma game shown in table 4.1. There are two players, each of which has two options: cooperate or defect. For example, in an employment context, player 1 could be a worker; to cooperate means to work hard, to defect means to shirk. For player 2, the employer, to cooperate means to provide a good working environment, to defect means otherwise. The numbers give the payoffs for each possibility (player 2's payoff is always on the left of the comma, player 1's payoff to the right). So if both cooperate, both get 5; if both defect both get 2. Note that for both to cooperate is the socially optimal result since 5 + 5 is the highest payoff of any of the joint decisions. If either player cooperates while the other defects, the cooperator gets 0 while the defector gets 6. The cooperator's payoff in that case is sometimes called the "sucker's payoff."

		Player 1	
		Cooperate	Defect
Player 2	Cooperate	5, 5	0, 6
	Defect	6, 0	2, 2

TABLE 4.1. Prisoner's Dilemma Game

It is important to be clear about what the payoffs represent. Sometimes they represent monetary amounts. Sometimes they represent the utility for each monetary payoff. Sometimes they represent the utility payoffs for each choice. The last interpretation includes all of the relevant preferences over any choice (e.g., guilt from defection). For purists only the third interpretation makes sense, and, when properly understood in this way, there can only be one solution to the game as described here.[1] For now, assume that the payoffs give the utility payoffs of the monetary amounts, and that that is the only relevant preference or consideration.

Prisoner's Dilemma games are noncooperative in that no binding commitments are possible. It would be in the joint interests of both players to somehow assure that both cooperate, but no binding contracts, bonds, or sunk costs exist to assist that goal. For instance, contracts may be too costly, or even if they were possible it is too uncertain whether a court would be able to make the correct determination, find for the aggrieved party, and enforce that decision. Given this context, what would each player do?

For game theorists, the question is what strategy would the players employ. A strategy profile specifies each decision for all contingencies. For instrumentally rational players a minimalist requirement is that they do not use dominated strategies, that is, ones that produce a lower expected (utility) payoff. If the game is played once, and if each player knows the payoffs and also that the other is instrumentally rational, the game has a determinate solution: both players will defect and get a payoff of 2 each.[2] To see why, consider player 2's decision problem. If player 1 cooperates, player 2 gets 5 by also cooperating, but 6 by defecting. If player 1 defects, player 2 gets 0 by cooperating and

1. See Binmore 1994, vol. 1.

2. Assuming away any further complications like the players are closely related and could split the loot later.

2 by defecting. Therefore player 2's dominant strategy is to defect because that strategy leads to a higher payoff no matter what player 1 does. All other strategies are dominated because they yield lower expected payoffs. The reasoning for player 1's decision is the same because the payoffs are symmetrical. The outcome in which both players defect also constitutes the famous Nash equilibrium. A Nash equilibrium exists when no player benefits by changing her action given the actions of others.

That instrumentally rational players could choose in a way that apparently contradicts their true interests has prompted enormous attention. Since we know that people really do cooperate sometimes, the choice seems to be either that there is some kind of logical error in the game or that the game does not really describe the contexts where cooperation is observed. As alluded to earlier, and as persuasively argued by Ken Binmore, when properly understood the apparent anomaly cannot be the result of faulty logic of the game. That conclusion follows almost directly from the assumptions. So that leaves the second alternative. One modeling strategy is to selectively relax one or more assumptions of the game.

For instance, cooperation can arise if the game is played indefinitely or there is uncertainty about when the game will end.[3] Now, three broad classes of best-response strategies exist: always defect, always cooperate, or alternate cooperation with defection.[4] Suppose that at some arbitrary time period either the players know the game will be repeated in the next period, as in the indefinitely repeated case, or there is some sufficient probability that it will be played again. Player 2's best strategy may be to defect, based on player 1's play in the previous period. Player 1's best response, based on his strategy, may be to then defect in the current period. If that was player 1's best response in the current period it will be same in the next if player 2 again defects. Thus "always defect" could be an equilibrium strategy. But so too could strategies that lead to "always cooperate." If in some arbitrary period player 2 cooperates,

3. Perhaps counterintuitively, cooperation cannot arise in a finitely repeated Prisoner's Dilemma game if it is only repeated a very large number of times. Say the same exact game is played a billion times. To find out how rational players would play this kind of repeated game, game theorists first look at the last play of the game. Note that the last round is exactly equivalent to a one-shot game because there is no next round. Therefore rational players defect for the same reason they would defect in a one-shot game. How about play in the second to last period? Since each knows that the other will defect in the next (that is, last) period, neither reputation nor future threats of defection could matter, so rational players will defect in this round as well. The same reasoning applies to the third to the last round, the fourth to the last round and all the way back to the first round. Backward induction dictates that rational players (who know the rationality of the other) defect in each and every round of a finitely repeated Prisoner's Dilemma game.

4. In fact, the Folk Theorem in game theory says that any such payoffs can result from some best response strategies. See Sugden 1986; Hargreaves Heap and Varoufakis 1995.

and player 1's best strategy dictates cooperation as a response, then the same will occur in the next period provided player 2 again cooperates.

The famous tit-for-tat strategy provides a good example of an alternating-response strategy. In that strategy the player starts the first period with cooperation and then always mimics what her partner did in the previous period. It is the ultimate expression of reciprocity. So if player 2 cooperates in the last period, player 1 cooperates in the current period, and vice versa. If both players are strictly faithful to the strategy, then both will cooperate indefinitely. However, if one deviates, through some simple mistake (called a "trembling hand" by game theorists) for instance, both players could find themselves in an endless chain of alternating "cooperate now, defect next period" play. In any case, if there is sufficient probability of play in the next period, the tit-for-tat strategy can be a best reply to itself. Tit-for-tat type strategies with the possibility of a next period work because defecting behavior by a partner now can be punished later. The threat of future retaliation serves as a deterrent. And cooperation now is rewarded with cooperation in the next period.

The use of a tit-for-tat strategy also reveals how cooperation can emerge in even finitely repeated Prisoner's Dilemma games. Instrumental rationality dictates that players always defect in finitely repeated Prisoner's Dilemma games so long as each player knows of the other's instrumental rationality. Suppose instead that there was some positive probability that one player, say player 2, was a hard-core tit-for-tat type. Perhaps player 2 was hardwired by evolutionary forces to act that way (we will come back to that possibility later). If player 1 is instrumentally rational she will certainly defect in the last period of the game regardless of player 2's type. But the uncertainty about player 2's type implies that player 1 may cooperate in earlier periods in order to gain the higher payoffs from cooperation. Interestingly, even if player 2 is not a tit-for-tat type player, the uncertainty confronted by player 1 may induce player 2 to fake being a tit-for-tat type player, at least for a little while. The possibility that player 2 could cooperate early on either because she is a true tit-for-tat type player or because she is faking it could induce player 1 to cooperate as well. Thus, if the probability that player 2 is a tit-for-tat player is sufficient, player 2 will cooperate, at least for awhile. Of course, if and when player 2 defects she reveals herself not to be a tit-for-tat player, and player 1 defects in the next period with certainty regardless of any previous or planned future play.

The mystery remains as to why it is the case that people do cooperate in *one-shot* social dilemma games, where reciprocity is impossible. Robyn Dawes and his colleagues offer an evolution-based explanation.[5] They introduce the notion of *sociality*—an evolutionary selection process that favors individuals who work well in groups. The idea is that humans were never solitary creatures and always increased their chances of survival with group membership. Even with the reduced survival threats of today, traits that favor cooperation persist and can be activated with the act of communication. Most evolutionary scholars remain skeptical of group selection mechanisms.[6]

Another set of explanations come from philosophers and philosophically minded economists. For instance, philosopher Margaret Gilbert introduces the notion of a *plural subject*, which is the body formed by individuals who jointly commit to something.[7] The idea takes *we* as a serious concept and does not rely on any kind of formal agreement. If individuals jointly intend to do something (like cooperate) as *we*, however, each individual has reason to do so. Amartya Sen introduced similar ideas earlier, by focusing on identity formation.[8] It is not surprising to see cooperation with others if individuals include in their identities others in their community or group, however defined. One way of interpreting these ideas is to say that an individual sometimes includes others' welfare into her own utility function. Finally, Hollis and Sugden suggest that Prisoner's Dilemma situations could be solved if individuals use the kind of Kantian internalist reasoning described in the previous chapter.[9] Of course that solution would require the context to be one where some kind of moral imperative was at stake. It is unclear how games without communication would qualify. However, contexts where individuals make verbal agreements do qualify, and, with the aid of preference-integrity, that is the case the next section seeks to develop. Most fundamentally, it will be a preference to "not lie" rather than the welfare of others that drives the analysis.

4.2. Preference-Integrity and Lying in Game Theory

In a standard social dilemma game pre-play communication does not matter to the extent that it misrepresents an agent's true interests.[10] In the one-shot

5. See, for instance, Caporael et al. 1989.
6. For instance, see the response by Tooby and Cosmides (1989) to the Caporael et al. 1989 target article.
7. Gilbert 1989.
8. Sen 1985.
9. Hollis and Sugden 1993.
10. Some of this material is adapted from the more general treatment in Minkler and Miceli 2004.

Prisoner's Dilemma game, if player 1 tells player 2 that she will cooperate by not confessing, player 2 will properly discount such utterances as cheap talk because she knows that it contradicts player 1's dominant strategy of defecting (confessing). There are only two requirements. First, the payoffs in table 4.1 must represent the preferences from each choice. Second, there must be common knowledge of each player's instrumental rationality. The players could benefit if they were able to make binding agreements, but since they cannot each is confident that utterances by the other are lies.

Economists typically don't consider lies, but in this case if they did they would just say that any cost of lying would already be accounted for in the (utility) payoffs. The trouble with this kind of response is that lying never matters and never allows persons of integrity to keep their word in a social dilemma–type setting. One way of addressing that shortcoming is with an analysis that includes the existence of persons on an integrity continuum, from those where there is little or no cost to lying to those for whom the cost may be great.

We can capture this idea by explicitly specifying a simple utility function that includes a monetary payoff (wealth) and also the possibility of a disutility associated with lying. If sufficient, the disutility represents the reason for the person of preference-integrity not to lie. The utility function takes the form:

$$(1)\ U_i = \begin{cases} W_i \text{ if cooperate} \\ W_i - x_i \text{ if defect.} \end{cases}$$

W_i is the wealth payoff to person i, which also depends on what the other person does. Now the payoffs in table 4.1 give the relevant *wealth* payoffs. Assume that the context is one where an agreement is being made, and that the agents make representations about what they will do, in this case to cooperate, so that to actually cooperate *also* means to tell the truth. There is no disutility from telling the truth, so the payoff only includes wealth. In contrast, if the agent defects, her total utility includes her material payoff, W_i, and also the disutility of lying, x_i. To include the notion of a continuum of preference-integrity, assume that x varies randomly across players. For this example, as62sume that x is uniformly distributed on the interval [0,3]; it has equal chance to be any value between 0 and 3 and its mean is 1.5. If $x = 0$ the agent attaches no utility cost to lying, but for the agent whose $x = 3$ there is significant cost. Intermediate x's reflect different intensities of preference-integrity.

While promising does not play much of a role in the typical analysis, it plays a central role here. If an agent of preference-integrity promises to cooperate or fulfill an agreement's obligations without ever intending to, that person is a liar. Such representations are not just cheap talk. Therefore, the possibility of making promises has to be explicitly included into the analysis. To do so, we include an initial stage, stage 1, in which the agents choose whether or not to make promises. After this decision, they then choose to cooperate or defect in stage 2. Define the indicator function, y, to reflect an agent's promising strategy in stage 1.

$$(2)\ y_j = \begin{cases} 1, \text{ if agent } j \text{ promised to cooperate in stage 1.} \\ 0, \text{ if agent } j \text{ did not promise to cooperate in stage 1.} \end{cases}$$

The indicator function describes whether the cost of lying becomes relevant. If agent j does not promise to cooperate in stage 1, $y = 0$, and there can be no disutility associated with lying if she chooses to defect in stage 2.

The payoffs from the modified stage 2 game are given in table 4.2. Provided that they promised in stage 1, note that players suffer a disutility (if $x > 0$) from lying no matter what their partner does. Preference-integrity is different from reciprocity because here liars suffer disutility even if playing with other liars. The relevant dimension is the act of lying upon one's own welfare. In contrast, on moral grounds at least, reciprocity makes one's own behavior the prisoner of another's character defects.[11] In that case, lying to a liar constitutes punishment or revenge. Still, if the probability of playing with a liar appears great, there should be (moral) options. One such option that we include in the following analysis is the possibility that an agent can *exit* the relationship before playing the stage 2 game, after observing whether or not her partner made a promise to cooperate in stage 1. That option helps the person

		Player 1	
		Cooperate	Defect
Player 2	Cooperate	5, 5	$0, 6 - y_1x_1$
	Defect	$6 - y_2x_2, 0$	$2 - y_2x_2, 2 - y_1x_1$

TABLE 4.2. Stage 2 of Modified Prisoner's Dilemma Game

11. Bok 1978, 127. Nevertheless, reciprocity has become quite popular in economics. See, for instance, Fehr and Gächter 2000b.

of integrity avoid being "played for a sucker" by keeping her own promise with a probable liar, while at the same time not forcing her to take the perceived immoral action of lying herself.

Assume that each agent knows y_j, that is, each knows if the other made a promise in stage 1. That certainly makes sense for the case of agreements. We also assume that while each agent knows her own x, she cannot reliably communicate its value to the other. That also makes sense for contexts in which the agents do not know one another (e.g., experimental games) or do not know one another well (most people who perceive the need for agreements). We do assume that the players know the distribution of x, however, so they can make certain conjectures about their partner's x given their (stage 1) behavior. Note that if $y = 1$ for at least one player (i.e., at least one promised to cooperate), the stage 2 game is no longer a Prisoner's Dilemma, and mutual defection is no longer guaranteed.

The game so far described is a game of incomplete information. To see what happens we begin by deriving the stage 2 outcomes and then consider optimal stage 1 strategies.[12] Consider the stage 2 pairings, given the history of play to that point. The first pairing consists of players neither of whom made a stage 1 promise (i.e., $y_1 = y_2 = 0$). In that case the payoff matrix in table 4.2 reduces to the Prisoner's Dilemma one in table 4.1. Thus each player employs the dominant strategy and defects, yielding a payoff of 2 to each. That payoff gives a reasonable exit option. We assume that before stage 2 begins, the players are entitled to exit the relationship and receive the same payoff as they would in the Prisoner's Dilemma game. It seems reasonable to assume that agents entering an agreement have outside options, the payoff of which is at least equal to the (defect, defect) payoff from the Prisoner's Dilemma game. As mentioned previously, that option also assures that players need not be played for suckers or sacrifice their preference-integrity. Given this specific exit option, each of the two nonpromising players is indifferent between playing the stage 2 game and exiting prior to stage 2.

Now consider the pairing of two players both of whom promise to cooperate (i.e., $y_1 = y_2 = 1$). Now the x's matter. Since each knows her own x but not the other's, each must calculate the probability, p, that their (randomly chosen) partner will cooperate, given that both players promised to do so. Given p, the expected payoff from cooperating is shown in equation (3).

(3) $U_c = 5p + 0(1 - p) = 5p.$

12. Technically, we seek a perfect Bayesian equilibrium of the overall game, which is just a Nash equilibrium of a dynamic game with incomplete information. See Gibbons 1992, chapter 4, for discussion of the equilibrium concept.

The expected payoff from defecting (lying) is shown in equation (4).

$$(4)\ U_d = p(6 - x) + (1 - p)(2 - x) = 4p + 2 - x.$$

A player therefore cooperates if $U_c > U_d$, or:

$$(5)\ x > 2 - p.$$

We can differentiate players into distinct three distinct types based on (5). The lowest value the right-hand side (RHS) of the inequality can take is 1 if $p = 1$. That means that the partner will cooperate with certainty. But so long as $x < 1$, the player will lie and defect even with known cooperators. Of course low x's indicate a low preference for truth-telling, or low or nonexistent preference-integrity. In contrast, the highest value the RHS of the inequality could take is 2 if $p = 0$. That means the partner will defect and lie with certainty. But so long as $x > 2$, the player will tell the truth and cooperate even with known defectors. Such players possess high preference-integrity. That leaves the third group, those with $1 > x > 2$ whose strategy depends on the equilibrium value of p, which is yet to be determined. This group possesses intermediate preference-integrity. To recap, high preference-integrity players ($x > 2$) always keep their promises and cooperate (if they proceed to stage 2). Low preference-integrity types ($x < 1$) always lie and defect. Intermediate preference-integrity types ($1 > x > 2$) base their strategy on the estimated probability of their partner's type.

The third possible stage 2 pairing involves a player who promised to cooperate and one who did not. If player 1 makes the promise, then $y_1 = 1$ and $y_2 = 0$ in the payoff matrix in table 4.2. Consider player 2's strategy first. For any p, the player defects if $U_d > U_c$, or:

$$(6)\ 4p + 2 > 5p.$$

Since (6) holds for all p, defection is the dominant strategy for a nonpromising player.

Now consider the optimal strategy of the promisor, player 1, in this pairing. Since she knows about (6), she rationally calculates that $p = 0$, that is, player 2 will defect with certainty. From (5), we know that a promisor will cooperate if $x > 2$. As noted earlier, only players with high preference-integrity meet this condition. But this player can do even better by exiting prior to the start of stage 2 because in that case she can receive a payoff of 2. The possibility of exit means that player 1 does not have to accept the "sucker's payoff" of

0 if playing against a known defector. In effect, the promisor switches her stage 1 strategy by retracting her promise. Thus the "promise–don't promise" pairing will never proceed to stage 2.

To this point we have shown that the only pairs that might proceed to the stage 2 game are those that either both promise to cooperate, or those who don't. Those who don't make promises will only find other players who do likewise, whereas promisors are only willing to partner with other promisors. The next question is what strategy players will rationally adopt in stage 1, given the feasible pairings and payoffs from the stage 2 game.

First consider the player who, if she promises to cooperate in stage 1, finds it optimal to lie and defect in stage 2 (i.e., $U_d > U_c$ given p). Such a player may receive an even higher payoff by not making a promise in stage 1. This type of player prefers not to promise in stage 1 and instead partners with another nonpromisor if $2 > U_d$, or if $x > 4p$. Otherwise, if $x < 4p$ then the player finds it optimal to lie and defect.

Next consider the player who honors her stage 1 promise and cooperates in the stage 2 game (i.e., $U_c > U_d$ given p). This player might receive an even higher payoff by not making a stage 1 promise and partnering with another stage 1 nonpromisor if $2 > U_c$, or if $p < 2/5$. Note that this choice does not depend on the player's type. If $p > 2/5$, the player always finds it optimal to make a stage 1 promise and cooperate in the stage 2 game.

This last condition is crucial. It shows that no player will cooperate in the stage 2 game if $p < 2/5$ because none finds it optimal to promise to cooperate in stage 1. Thus we need to find the equilibrium p to the overall game to see if cooperation and truth-telling exist. We now know that such a condition requires that $p > 2/5$ so that stage 2 cooperators are willing to make stage 1 promises. Also, in order to align conjectures, the equilibrium p must equal the true fraction of cooperators in stage 2 so that expectations are fulfilled. Using (5), this requires that:

$$(7)\ p = Pr(x > 2 - p).$$

Since x is uniformly distributed on [0,3], (7) becomes $p = [3 - (2p)]/3$. Solving yields $p^* = 1/2$. This finding means that *all* players make a promise to cooperate in stage 1 and then play the stage 2 game with a randomly chosen player.[13] No players exit. In the stage 2 game 1/2 of the players cooperate,

13. See Minkler and Miceli 2004 for the general conditions for this result to hold. The analysis there establishes the necessary conditions on x, given the payoffs of a Prisoner's Dilemma game, for cooperation to exist.

those with $x > 2 - p^*$, or $x = 1.5$, while 1/2 lie and defect. Those with low preference-integrity ($x < 1$) always lie and defect. Those with high preference-integrity ($x > 2$) always keep their promises and cooperate.

The intermediate preference-integrity group ($1 < x < 2$) is the interesting one. One half of that group ($1 < x < 1.5$) act like the low preference-integrity types; they lie and defect. In contrast, the other half ($1.5 < x < 2$) act like the high preference-integrity types; they keep their promises and cooperate. So while there are three discernible types of players, there are only two strategy profiles used. The payoffs for each strategy are determined by using (3) and (4). Those who keep their promise and cooperate receive $U_c = 2.5$. Those who lie and defect get $U_d = 4 - x$, which is equal to or greater than 2.5 given that only those with $x < 1.5$ use this strategy. Thus the expected payoffs are higher in equilibrium when compared to the one-shot Prisoner's Dilemma game and its equilibrium of mutual defection. A sufficient amount of integrity results in higher payoffs by promoting a critical amount of cooperation.[14]

At this point some might protest about the result that low preference-integrity types get at least as much utility as high preference-integrity types. Those attracted to evolutionary analyses in particular might ask how such payoffs could be sustained over time. There are two types of responses. First, since the model seeks to describe contexts where agreements are central, we can suppose that survival needs have already been met. The benefits from agreements constitute a surplus beyond what is needed for an adequate survival. This surplus is the player's subjective evaluation of wealth plus being truthful.

The second response makes direct use of evolutionary analysis, as in the work of Robert Frank, discussed in chapter 1. Suppose for some reason that over time evolutionary pressures dictated that utility among all types had to be equated in equilibrium. While not modeled here, one could easily envision such a scenario if the assumption about players not being able to communicate their x's was dropped. Note that if the x's were perfectly observable, high preference-integrity types would only couple with each other and, since they would never defect, would always get a material payoff of 5. All other types would get a lesser payoff, and by evolutionary reasoning, they would perish. Only high preference-integrity types would survive (i.e., $p = 1$). In contrast, suppose that high preference-integrity types could intentionally couple with

14. Examples of other models that generate cooperation, but without communication, include Rabin 1993 with its emphasis on players' beliefs about their partner's intent and how fairness dictates reciprocity, and Fehr and Schmidt 1999, which posits a preference for inequity aversion. Dowell, Goldfarb, and Griffith 1998 provides a simple non-game-theoretic model that allows for promises by including a lumpy (0,1 indicator) preference for honesty in the utility function.

each other but only after incurring some detection cost. Now their expected material payoffs would be higher than 2.5, but less than 5. In that case other types of players could survive over time by getting the same payoff (the exact payoffs of all types would depend on the cost of detection). Since the detection cost is positive, some players with a high or intermediate x would not make the investment, and thus some liars would prey on those types.

Another objection might center on the assumption that those of preference-integrity suffer a utility loss if they lie to someone else who also lies. It cannot be emphasized enough that integrity is different than reciprocity: it is the act of lying itself that the person of preference-integrity seeks to avoid, because to do so would be utility reducing. Thus a person of preference-integrity would either exit in stage 1 or keep her promise if she advanced to stage 2.

Still, it is true that persons of integrity may sometimes find themselves in contexts of mutual deceit. Mutual deceit might occur when each person involved believes it acceptable to lie; games of poker and white lies to one's spouse to make them feel good are examples. Could the same be said about agreements? In general, the answer is no, because the permissibility of mutual deceit for persons of integrity hinges on the other believing that lying is acceptable. Certainly if one's partner makes a promise in stage 1 and then cooperates in stage 2, that constitutes decisive evidence that she did not think it acceptable to lie. But suppose one's partner does lie. That could simply mean that the partner had a sufficiently low x, as modeled earlier. It is at least conceivable, however, that the partner judged the context to be one where lying is permissible, maybe because "everyone does it" and it has become standard practice. In that case the negative effect of lying to a liar may be diminished.

Mutual deceit of this sort can be incorporated into the model by simply adding a parameter to represent the degree to which the players perceive the context to be one where lying is permissible. Doing so changes the payoffs in the lower right-hand cell of table 4.2 (where both players lie) to $2 - \alpha x$. If $\alpha = 1$, lying is not permissible and the game remains the one described. If $\alpha = 0$, the context is one where lying is widely accepted, and the payoffs become identical to those in a Prisoner's Dilemma game for that cell (i.e., defect, defect). If $0 \leq \alpha < 1$, the player perceives that the context is one in which mutual deceit is at least partially acceptable, and the "cost" of lying is diminished accordingly.[15] Thus for all $\alpha < 1$, more lying and defection result for any given distribution of preference-integrity. Stated differently, a strictly positive implies that more in-

15. The expected payoff from defecting (lying) becomes: (4′) $U_d = 4p + 2 - x(p - \alpha + \alpha p)$. The expected payoff from defecting is now greater than that found in (4) because $(p - \alpha + \alpha p) < 1$ for all $p < 1$.

tegrity is required to obtain the results reported here. So while most cases of promise making involve clear moral requirements, those that don't will result in more lying and less cooperation for any level of preference-integrity. But in cases of true mutual deceit, that would be of little consequence.

To summarize, we have shown that the notion of preference-integrity can be employed in simple game theory to describe contexts of agreements, and that doing so generates novel implications. If there is a continuum of the preference for honesty, three distinct preference-integrity types result: high, low, and intermediate. Though there are three types, each will employ only one of two strategies. High preference-integrity types always make stage 1 promises and then keep them by cooperating in stage 2. Their preference for honesty is decisive. These are the Don Quixotes of the model. Low preference-integrity types always make stage 1 promises and then lie and defect in stage 2 (the Volpones). These players' preference for material wealth dominates. Intermediate preference-integrity types follow stage 1 promises with either a kept promise or a lie, depending on their own value of x and the estimated probability that their partner will keep their promise. These Marthas balance their material and moral preferences. There must be a sufficient amount of preference-integrity in the population for players to make stage 1 promises, but if there is, all do.[16] Perhaps most important, promises do matter. Sometimes talk is golden, not cheap. Thus the model can explain both agreement keeping even in the face of countervailing material incentives and also why reputations are not necessary to sustain trust. Players keep their promises, not in order to build reputations that will instrumentally fulfill other objectives, but because they prefer to do so—as long as a sufficient number of other players prefer to do so as well.

The model also provides an explanation for the results found in the experimental literature: when people say they will contribute to a public good they often do so; to do otherwise would be to lie.[17] As mentioned in chapter 1,

16. Basu (2006) also finds cooperation in a modified Prisoner's Dilemma game, one that includes other-regarding behavior. He finds conditions such that a small perturbation, like adding one more noncooperator to a population, can lead to a cascade and a total breakdown of cooperation. The same is true for our model. If a sufficient number of high or intermediate honesty types switched to low honesty, such that $p < 2/5$, no player would make a promise in the first stage to cooperate in the second stage.

17. Minkler and Miceli (2004) extend the model to include another round of play; that is, the game is repeated. Provided that the players use an adaptive strategy, and each can observe what the other did in the first round of play, it turns out that cooperators continue to cooperate with first-period cooperators but would exit with first-period defectors, and defectors continue to defect with first-period defectors. If however we eliminate the assumption about exit, maybe because the players are locked into long-term contracts, it turns out that some who cooperated in the first period now defect with first-period defectors, but also that some first-period defectors now cooperate with first-

in his meta-analysis David Sally estimates that (noncredible) promises to cooperate elicited by experimenters increase cooperation by 12 to 30 percent.[18] What the model fails to do is to account for the empirical observation that the propensity to lie decreases with the perceived harm caused by lying.[19] That insight could be the target of future refinements.

4.3. Evolutionary Game Theory

Standard game theory has been criticized for a variety of reasons. The assumption of common knowledge about each player's (instrumental) rationality and the typical result of a multiplicity of equilibria are often the chief targets. The first refers to each player's ability to make complex calculations and inferences, and the knowledge that each has the ability and wish to do so. Overwhelming evidence indicates that people seldom employ the type of hyperrationality that game theorists assume.[20] Sometimes people act boundedly rational, at least partly because of the costs of deliberation. We employ simple rules and conventions to help solve complex problems. The second criticism refers to the many cases where games have multiple solutions and no convincing way to choose among them. Since games with multiple solutions can yield conflicting implications, their empirical applicability is severely compromised. These problems have led game theorists to explore other behaviors and contexts, culminating in the recent popularity of evolutionary game theory.[21]

Evolutionary game theory considers interactions over time. As its name further implies, all the models assume that evolutionary processes select out the most successful traits. Inevitably, these models also assume different kinds of behavioral foundations. Sometimes behavior is assumed to be genetically determined in a literal sense, in which case successful behavioral traits propagate through the reproductive successes of their carriers. At other times the biological process of evolution is used metaphorically. In these accounts traits refer to preferences, strategies, and behavior rules that are transmitted through learning and imitation. The most successful traits result in higher

period cooperators. This kind of switching behavior not only seems to exist in real life but also implies an important role for institutions in facilitating intentional interactions.

18. Sally 1995, 62.

19. Gneezy 2005.

20. See Conlisk 1996.

21. For good reviews of this literature, see Mailath 1998; Samuelson 2002; Sethi and Somanathan 2003.

payoffs. Culture, norms, and conventions often help to coordinate actions. As a simple example, no one finds it beneficial to drive on the left side of the road if all others drive on the right side. The literature suggests that in a wide variety of circumstances, conforming pays.

The notion of an *evolutionarily stable strategy* (ESS) is one of the hallmarks of evolutionary game theory.[22] Consider a large population of agents who repeatedly engage in random (say, Prisoner's Dilemma–like) interactions. Natural selection favors those who employ strategies with higher average payoffs over time. Higher payoffs imply higher rates of reproduction, for instance. An incumbent strategy that is widespread in the population is said to be an ESS if it can repel any sufficiently small entry by mutants. An ESS exists if either (1) the mutant strategy earns a lower payoff against the incumbent strategy than the incumbent strategy does against itself, or (2) the mutant earns the same against the incumbent as the incumbent does against itself, but the mutant earns less against itself than the incumbent earns against the mutant.

The initial hope was that ESS could address at least one of the problems of standard game theory by producing a unique equilibrium. However, it turns out that there are many contexts for which no strategy is stable. The repeated Prisoner's Dilemma is one such case. To see why, consider three popular strategies. First assume that "always cooperate" was widespread in the population. Then the mutant "always defect" could always get a foothold and propagate since that strategy gets a higher payoff when pairing with an "always cooperate" type.

The next two scenarios are less obvious. Now assume that a tit-for-tat type strategy (cooperate on the first play, and then do what your partner did in the last period) was widespread. Since the strategy "always cooperate" gets the same payoff when playing with a tit-for-tat type or against itself, it could get a foothold (i.e., can't be repelled). Of course if it did, then the strategy "always defect" could also enter and propagate, resulting in further instability. Finally, suppose that the population initially consisted of "always defect" types. Now *tat*-for-tit types, those who defect in the first period and then change their action whenever their partner defects, can get a foothold because that strategy gets the same payoff as "always defect" when playing against that type, but does better against itself than "always defect" does against itself. Two tat-for-tit types initially defect, and then cooperate thereafter. Other mutant

22. The idea originated from Smith and Price 1972 and was developed further in Smith 1982, where the notion of a neutrally stable strategy (NSS), which is based on weaker assumptions, was also introduced.

strategies can imitate tat-for-tit types and hence get a foothold in that population. And so on. It turns out, however, that stability does exist when theorists employ the notion of a "neutrally stable strategy" with its weaker assumptions, but those results change once again if additional elements like complexity are added.[23] Not surprisingly, evolutionary game theory, like all theory, depends critically upon its underlying assumptions.

There are some very interesting models employing these evolution-based methods. Robert Frank considers a large population consisting of two types, those who always cooperate and those who always defect in a Prisoner's Dilemma interaction.[24] If interactions are random and players cannot identify each other's type, defectors eventually drive out all cooperators by virtue of their higher average payoffs. By contrast, if players could perfectly identify one another, cooperators would partner only with each other, and defectors would eventually die out because of their lower payoffs. Most interesting, Frank shows that if there is some positive cost of scrutinizing the other's type, then an evolutionarily stable equilibrium exists that includes both types (each type gets the same expected payoff). Defectors get a foothold because in a population with sufficiently high cooperation, some cooperators do not invest in scrutiny. Some defectors benefit from partnering with those cooperators, which then increases the average payoff to defectors. Frank also suggests that credible signals like emotional responses can help to reveal a partner's type. Investments in scrutiny help to address the problem of mimicry, that is, when defectors try to portray themselves as cooperators.

Other efforts focus on the role of culture. Boyd and Richerson first note the problem confronted by evolutionary biologists who try to understand cooperative human behavior by placing its origins in selfish genes.[25] The puzzle centers on why unrelated people living in large groups would cooperate with each other if cooperating involves a cost. The authors resolve the puzzle by positing that human behavior is a compromise between genetically determined selfish impulses and cooperative values acquired culturally. Culture transmits information about behavior that generates the highest payoffs in a

23. A neutrally stable strategy allows the mutant to mimic the incumbent strategy during the course of play. Using that criterion, tit-for-tat is a NSS. The strategy "always defect" is not because in the limit over time tit-for-tat types get at least as much. The addition of complexity costs changes the situation. Binmore and Samuelson (1992) assume that the simpler of two strategies otherwise giving the same payoffs has the evolutionary advantage. Now, the strategy "always cooperate" can get a foothold in a tit-for-tat population. In contrast, the tat-for-tit strategy is an NSS if there are complexity costs because it does better than both the "always defect" and more complicated imitator strategies.

24. Frank 1987, 1988.

25. Boyd and Richerson 1990.

given environment, and often conformity is an appropriate strategy to reduce the learning costs associated with finding favored behaviors. In fact, the explicit modeling of learning is another feature found throughout the evolutionary game theory literature and serves as another way of distinguishing it from standard game theory. Sometimes the benefits of employing simple rules to solve complex problems outweigh the costs of making mistakes.

Ken Binmore offers a most ambitious effort of evolutionary game theory to describe the social contract.[26] He argues that the "game of life" determines the feasible set of outcomes a society could achieve. The "game of morals" (social contract) is a coordination device to select among the equilibria in the feasible set. The equilibrium is self-enforcing in the sense that no one has the incentive to deviate from their anticipated behavior given what everyone else is doing. People imitate successful behavior and are moral in the sense that they reciprocate the actions of others. Imitation and reciprocity derive from the evolutionary advantages they have conferred throughout human history. Apparently, the relatively well-off will increasingly understand that it is in their own enlightened interests to share with those less fortunate because the latter largely determine the former's security. In Binmore's view, property rights are a social institution that could be changed if those less advantaged cease to give their consent. In sum, Binmore uses evolutionary game theory to give a naturalistic, relativistic account that tries to describe social outcomes and also the processes behind progressive social change.[27]

4.4. Integrity in Evolutionary Game Theory

What is evolutionary game theory's relationship to preference-integrity and commitment-integrity? The case of preference-integrity is relatively straightforward. To the extent that preference formation can be described by evolutionary forces, and those treating evolution as a metaphor seem most relevant so long as it's honesty being selected for, then preference-integrity fits nicely into the theory. Social institutions like education, religion, and civic groups do promote honesty, and since there are material benefits to honest people partnering with one another, we could expect institutions to evolve that

26. Binmore 1994, 1998.

27. While Binmore's tomes were generally well received, Sugden (2001) extensively criticizes the work as lacking support for its purported naturalistic foundations. I will consider the topic of naturalism presently. To the extent that Binmore's ultimate aim is to argue for social progress by giving those less well-off reason to respect the security of those more well-off, much simpler models achieve the same objective. See, for instance, Eaton and White 1991.

would facilitate such interactions. In any event, to the extent that individuals adopt a preference for honesty, then the analyses in chapter 2 and earlier in this chapter become pertinent. Evolutionary forces may not exhaust the ways in which individuals come to embrace a preference for honesty, but they provide one reasonable approach. The only thing to keep in mind is that honesty is different from reciprocity, whether modeled as a preference, strategy, or trait. How and why institutions select for reciprocity versus honesty are questions needing further study.

To the extent that preferences are subject to evolutionary forces, their effect on commitment-integrity has already been described in chapter 3. A person of commitment-integrity bases her decision to act honestly on her strength of will versus the utility benefit from lying. Such a person has chosen to identify with the commitment to some honesty principle, the minimalist principle "lying is wrong," for instance. The question is, can the person will her acts accordingly? That depends on the strength of their will versus the utility of lying. Anything that decreases the utility of lying, like evolutionary forces selecting the preference for honesty, increases the likelihood that any given will's strength will be sufficient to act.

The more difficult issue centers on the naturalistic nature of some evolutionary game theory. Naturalism usually considers ethical propositions as either deriving from natural phenomena (scientific, perhaps biological) or as vacuous. Those embracing naturalism in evolutionary game theory, like Ken Binmore, think it meaningless to talk of acts or reasons for acts as being good or right. Instead, individuals are envisioned to imitate and learn through trial and error, and to follow reciprocity-based conventions. Biological and social processes (genes and memes) select for those that are fit and weed out the weak. What is crucial is that individual behavior is assumed to be completely determined by such processes. Binmore is unabashed about the implications of such a project: in his view, there is no such thing as a free will.[28] Clearly, without the possibility of a free will, or more precisely, conscious reflection, the concept of commitment-integrity would be impossible. Thus, naturalist models that treat preferences, strategies, and/or traits as stemming *exclusively* from evolutionary forces beyond an individual's control, and also as the *only* possible source of behavior, are squarely at odds with the account I have offered of commitment-integrity, which requires choices based on conscious reflection and necessitates a free, if only weak, will. Of course those kinds of

28. See, for instance, Binmore 1994, 208–9. That is, if we knew the precise workings of a decision maker's mind, we could predict each and every decision with complete certainty.

naturalists need to provide an evolutionary rationale for conscious reflection, to my knowledge a project not yet achieved.

One need not be a purist in this debate. The notion of commitment-integrity does include preferences, and, as noted here, those preferences could certainly derive from evolutionary processes. So while commitment-integrity is inconsistent with a hard-core naturalist project, it is consistent with evolutionary processes acting on preferences. It therefore is compatible with those who view both evolutionary processes *and* conscious reflection as important determinants of behavior, as Amartya Sen notes.

> There is no question whatsoever that the recent work on evolutionary theory, including the study of evolutionary games, has thrown much light on the way behavioral norms and values may get socially selected and manage to survive and flourish. The question that arises is not the need for taking note of evolutionary selection, which is clearly important. But once evolutionary survival is taken into account, must the burden of selection fall *entirely* on that process (with conscious selection reduced to simple endorsement of natural selection)? Why can't the two means of selection be both actively at work? Since human beings are reflective creatures who take their values and critical powers seriously, the role of conscious and scrutinized selection is also going on. Critical reflection does not give immunity from evolutionary selection, but nor does evolutionary selection convert reflective beings into thoughtless automatons.[29]

29. Sen 1998, x.

Chapter 5

Lying, Contracts, and Political Behavior

The previous three chapters provided the theoretical foundations for integrity. This chapter begins the discussion of how integrity, particularly commitment-integrity, works in different contexts. It deals with legal contracts, which turn out to be fairly straightforward, and then moves to a more nuanced area, the political agreement. Throughout my analysis of these types of agreements and those that follow I will continually focus on the roles of coherence, a normative condition of integrity, and mutual deceit, a moral loophole of lying, to generate novel implications. Though alluded to briefly, mutual deceit has not yet been discussed in any detail, so the chapter starts by considering lying, the issue underlying the minimalist moral principle, and mutual deceit.

Don Quixote the politician keeps every promise he makes and upholds every contract he signs, even if it kills him. Volpone breaks political and contractual promises any time it suits him. Martha vows not to lie and even possesses the strength of will necessary to hold to that principle. Does that mean she could never break a contractual or political promise to remain a person of integrity?

5.1. Lying and Mutual Deceit

An untold number of philosophers throughout the ages have concerned themselves with the issue of "truth," yet the issue of lying has apparently garnered far less attention. Sissela Bok's work stands out as the contemporary classic on the issue and provides the basis for most of this section.[1]

Bok defines a lie as "an intentionally deceptive message in the form of a

1. Bok 1978.

statement."[2] Both the intent to deceive and the communication of the deception must exist. Intent is particularly crucial because it means that the liar knows she is trying to alter or bias the options of the person being lied to. As a result, lying yields three kinds of effects. First and foremost it harms those being lied to. Lying is like violence in that it can coerce individuals to act against their will. Second, it breaks down societal trust. To the extent that individuals cannot determine the veracity of claims made by those with whom they interact, fewer potentially beneficial interactions will occur. It is a bit of a paradox that market economies thrive on trust because it reduces the contracting and enforcement costs of interactions, but also that individuals confront the incentive to free ride on that trust because doing so could lead to material gains. If you entrust me with an asset without incurring legal protections, we may both gain by that reduced cost of our interaction, but I may also be tempted to violate your trust and skip town if it was my best economic alternative.[3] Moreover, the more it is perceived that those in the media, politics, and other major institutions lie, the less citizens will trust those institutions, and the less civic engagement results. A bandwagon of dishonesty could result, exhibiting a cascading effect similar to those that drive fads, sudden revolutions, and the spread of corruption.[4] Finally, while a liar usually lies in order to gain power or some other benefit, personal costs also exist. Not only does a liar risk losing personal credibility with others, but also a current lie may launch one down the slippery slope of making it easier to lie again. That's significant because lying generally diminishes one's own character. With a few possible exceptions to be discussed, a person who intends to harm or coerce others indulges traits that literally no moral, religious, or humanistic tradition endorses.

To consider the justifications for lying, we need to investigate two conditions: intent and alternatives. Lying with the intent to benefit oneself at the expense of harm or coercion to another brings about universal condemnation. In other cases, the issue of intent has proven to be more contentious.

Kant maintained that it is an absolute moral duty to not lie, no matter any goodness of intent. Based upon the three versions of the categorical imperative, we can deduce that a lie (1) is not a personal maxim that could be willed into a universal law, (2) would violate the dignity of the person lied to,

---

2. Bok 1978, 15.
3. The usual retort is that reputations or some other kind of sunk cost could prevent that act from being my best alternative. For the context of assuring product quality in a buyer-seller relationship, see Klein and Leffler 1980; Shapiro 1983. For a response that shows that reputations are not generally sufficient and that seller honesty is also required, see Adler 1992.
4. See Bikchandani, Hirshleifer, and Welsh 1992; Kuran 1995; Basu 2006.

and (3) is inconsistent with living in the realm of ends (perfectly moral world). For Kant, to lie is to violate the moral law and to thus harm humanity itself. Kant dismisses arguments that suggest lying may sometimes be justified if the intent is to prevent harm. Kant would say that we should not even lie to the man wishing to do harm to a child because we can only be responsible for our own actions, and we have the absolute duty of truthfulness. If the man harms the child it is his responsibility, not ours.[5] Some religious followers take similarly absolutist positions, St. Augustine, for instance.

But the issue of intent is relevant for others. The paradigmatic case is the one just mentioned, where the intent of a lie is to prevent harm. Many would argue that a person who plans harm has no *right* to truth when it comes to information that will aid his plan.[6] Since the planner of harm can claim no right to truth because he has no right to commit harm, the respondent has no duty to tell the truth, especially if a lie could thwart nefarious plans. Most people would find this kind of reasoning attractive.

It might seem that the intent to punish could also constitute another justification for lying. For instance, it might seem that lying to a liar is justified for the purpose of punishment. Many notions of fairness are based on reciprocity: cooperate with cooperators, defect with defectors, tell the truth to truth-tellers, lie to liars, and so on. The liar deserves what he gives. Certainly this is the tack of many social scientists.[7] But as Bok points out, lies can harm the liar, the lied to, and overall trust in society. She points to Vietnam and Watergate as key factors that precipitously eroded public trust among U.S. citizens. Most fundamentally, however, by resorting to reciprocity one also becomes a slave to the character flaws of another. To lie to another just because he is a liar makes the liar the author of our own actions. If instead the intent of lying to a liar would *also* prevent harm, then the prevention of harm would be its justification, not punishment.

Instead of punishment, it might be argued that the intent of lying is to

5. Many find this kind of case troubling. Ross (1939) deals with it by introducing the notion of prima facie duties. While duties cannot conflict, prima facie duties can. In the case of the child, the person being asked the location of the child confronts two prima facie duties: not lying and preventing harm. At the time of decision only one prima facie duty will reveal itself as a duty. Buddhists could offer another response based upon the precept of skillful speech, or speech that doesn't contribute to suffering. One could simply remain silent.

6. Kant would not make this argument because he believed both rights and duties to be universal. On this very point he writes, "First . . . truth is not a possession the right to which can be granted to one man but refused to another. But, secondly, he will not do so mainly because the duty of truthfulness (which is the only thing under consideration here) makes no distinction between persons to whom one has this duty and to whom one can be excused from this duty; it is, rather, an unconditional duty which holds in all circumstances" (1785, 66).

7. For two representative examples, see Rabin 1993; Fehr and Gächter 2000a, 2000b.

teach the liar a lesson, but there are alternatives to that approach. If one intends to teach the liar why he shouldn't lie, one could point to any number of religious or philosophical teachings. One could patiently explain how lying harms others, breaks down societal trust, and even harms the liar himself. One could often do that if one really intended to *teach* the liar a lesson. But if "teaching" is really just code for indulging punishment from the motive of revenge, then it is beset with the objections just given.

For the kinds of contexts I've been considering, Bok suggests a useful criterion to evaluate intent and hence whether a particular instance of lying is justified, which is to bring the case before reasonable people. This fictional device resembles Adam Smith's impartial spectator; one can stand apart from oneself to consider potential actions. Reasonable people would consider the harm that could be prevented by a lie, and also any available alternative to lying. Reasonable people would likely excuse a lie that prevents great harm, even in the face of the alternative of silence; they would not excuse lying, even to a liar, if the prevention of some overriding harm was not at stake, and if alternatives to lying were available.

Most lying in economic contexts, however, occurs for personal gain. A seller who intentionally lies to a buyer in order to increase her profits does not in any meaningful way intend to prevent harm or even teach the buyer a lesson. Reasonable people would have no difficulty in judging these kinds of lies as wrong, and a liar will generally know that. Still, there is one important qualification left to consider, namely, what Bok calls mutual deceits. Such deceits are usually deemed "acceptable." They are important because an important question centers on whether a person of integrity can ever justify lying in the types of agreements considered in this book.

Mutual deceits are lies that do not carry any moral force, such as bluffs in poker and white lies to partners.[8] There are two conditions. First, everyone must know the rules of the game. Your wife must know you will say that the dress makes her look thin (and wants you to), just as you know she will say that your beer belly looks distinguished. Everyone who plays poker knows that lying wildly is the norm. The second condition requires that everyone *accepts* the rules of the game. It is hard to imagine someone becoming indignant at poker liars, but it is not hard to imagine spouses "wanting it straight." Some do, some don't. But in order for lying to be a case of mutual deceit, there must be *mutual* acceptance. Otherwise, there is harm. A wife who wants the truth even if the husband thinks a lie would be more kind has been harmed because

8. As discussed in the introduction, some psychologists think that most lying takes this form (see DePaulo et al. 1996).

her beliefs and actions have been biased by an insincere representation. Furthermore, if she finds out that it was a lie when she wanted truth, her level of trust will fall.

The challenge is to figure out which are true or real cases of mutual deceit. If individuals do not know the rules of the game or if they do not accept them, it's not mutual deceit. The buyer-seller context in economics is particularly important. Some "spot exchange" markets could be said to be characterized by mutual deceit. In flea markets and bazaars everyone knows and accepts that sellers underreport their true willingness-to-accept, and buyers underreport their true willingness-to-pay, at least initially. The used car market has historically been one where it is known that at least some sellers lie. Even if buyers do not explicitly accept those conditions, by entering into that market they implicitly do. Interestingly, economists typically characterize all markets as if they were of this sort. When modeling buyer-seller markets of any type, it is standard practice *not* to include reasons or preferences against lying (or any reasons for that matter).[9] By modeling all economic agents as instrumentally rational (with only material preferences), all talk becomes hot air or cheap talk, just as in cases of mutual deceit.

But it is clear that many, perhaps most, markets could not be said to be characterized by mutual deceit. Mutuality is the key. Most often, buyers do not want sellers to lie, and sellers know that, and sellers do not want buyers to lie, and buyers know that. The reason each party knows the other's wishes is that in such contexts decisions based on lies cause harm. Even if it is not often said "I do not want you to lie in our transaction because it will hurt me," indignation, real or potential, provides a reliable signal of harm and thus of the absence of mutuality. People typically don't get worked up if, based on a misrepresentation, they buy a bad blender at a flea market, because their decision to buy was not based on the lie; but they do get indignant if, contrary to promises, their employer (the buyer of their labor services) lays them off or changes their benefits. Those kinds of lies influence the decisions of those lied to (employees) and do cause harm.[10]

To further work with this minimalist moral principle of "lying is wrong" and mutual deceit, consider two different kinds of cases: legal contracts and political agreements.

9. Though the cost of reputational damage is often modeled in repeated interactions.

10. Still, as we will see in the next chapter, if some workplace was in fact characterized by lying on all sides, then perhaps it could be a place of mutual deceit. In that case, the potential for mutually beneficial exchanges is reduced.

5.2. Legal Contracts

Legal contracts specify the terms and conditions of legal promises.[11] The promises are legal in the sense that the parties can resort to courts to assure that they are kept, or, if not, proper damages are assessed. Economists view legal contracts as welfare enhancing because they facilitate voluntary exchange. So long as it is truly voluntary, and so long as it does not adversely affect third parties, an exchange must make the parties better off (or have the expectation that they will be better off) because otherwise they would not have agreed in the first place. The problem is that often the contingencies surrounding exchanges can get quite complex, making the writing and execution of contracts mediating those exchanges equally complex and potentially quite costly. In order to fully reflect each party's wishes, a complete contract would have to address all possible (relevant) circumstances, many of which could be unforeseen at the time of the contract. The court can provide the missing terms by relying on established doctrine and/or trying to infer the party's intent, but the necessary existence of incomplete contracts means that sometimes a contractual party will believe that she has been wronged—that a promise has been broken. The question, then, is what are the requirements for a person of integrity in terms of legal promises?

The first issue concerns intent. If an individual makes a promise, but never intended to keep the promise, then she is a liar. A contractual party who lies commits fraud. Fraud, therefore, occurs whenever one party intentionally deceives another about the quality or price of a good or service. Both the law and the ethical requirements for a person of integrity are clear in such a case. Courts take a dim view of fraud, will not generally recognize fraudulent contracts, and may significantly penalize deceivers. As for persons of integrity who commit to the minimalist principle that "lying is wrong," coherence requires them not to commit contractual fraud.

Seemingly less clear-cut is the case when a contractual party intends to keep a legal promise, but fails to do so because of some unforeseen contingency. The law considers such a case a breach and provides various legal remedies. The most common remedy is expectation damages, monetary compensation meant to leave the aggrieved party as well off as if the contract had been honored. At other times the court may impose other types of damages or require specific performance by the party in breach. In principle, a sufficient remedy could completely compensate the aggrieved party while the breach still improves overall welfare. For instance, suppose that buyer *A* contracts

11. For an economic analysis of contract law, see Miceli 1997; Shavell 2003.

with builder *B* to build a house for 100. Conceivably *A* could contract with another builder, but likes *B* 10 more than the next favored one (who also bid 100). At the time of the contract *B* estimates the cost of the project to be 90. Once beginning, however, it turns out that his best worker is injured and that to complete the project will cost 120. If the builder complies with the contract the net surplus is –10 (*A*'s surplus of 10 from using the preferred builder plus the loss to *B*). If *B* instead breaches and pays *A*'s expectation damages, leaving *A* as well off as if the contract had been fulfilled, total net welfare increases to 0 (*A*'s damages of 10 plus *B*'s cost of 10). The question is, was *B* wrong to breach and, if so, in what sense?

Steven Shavell argues that such a breach is not morally wrong, and legal scholars who believe otherwise are confused about the nature of an incomplete contract (and, by extension, legal promises).[12] Since an incomplete contract leaves some of the parties' wishes unspecified, the parties themselves would want compensatory damages in the event of a breach. That's how they would want to complete the contract. A broken promise only matters if the aggrieved party is left worse off (harmed), but since damages can make that party "whole," a breach is not only not immoral, oftentimes it will be efficient, as in the preceding case.

The reasoning for a person of integrity is somewhat similar. Assuming the minimalist conception, the issue hinges on the requirements for the person of integrity after a contract has been signed and after an unforeseen contingency has arisen. Intent is not the issue because even if the person of integrity breaches, it was not her intent to initially do so and it was not her intent to deceive. The matter turns more on context. Legal promises in commercial contexts are somewhat different than others because the parties do know that nonperformance is a possibility, and in that eventuality damages could compensate. These rules of the game are known by one and all. The situation is a weaker version of mutual deceit because everyone knows that legal promise breaking (but not lying) can occur due to unforeseen contingencies, and thus there exists the possibility of nonperformance. It is accepted as a risk of doing business. So as long as there was sincere intent to perform, a person of integrity could breach without loss of coherence *as long as sufficient damages are also paid.* Assuming this kind of breach and remedy, the aggrieved party suffers no economic harm in this commercial setting, the breaching party suffers no "character" harm because there was no intent to deceive, and the overall level of trust was unchanged because of the absence of these harms. Of course the analysis would be different if the person of integrity em-

12. Shavell 2003, 13.

braces a stronger principle, like "all promise-breaking is wrong," which would subsume the minimalist principle and additionally impose a stronger requirement. Context would be irrelevant, and coherence would require that person of integrity to fulfill the contract's terms no matter the unforeseen contingency. That unrealistic and onerous burden would also induce such persons to enter fewer contracts in the first place.

The analysis of contractual agreements is fairly clear-cut because by their nature they are explicit, and courts exist to help adjudicate unforeseen contingencies, breaches, and fraud. Sometimes the rules of the game are less clear. For instance, the next chapter discusses the employment agreement, an important case of contracts that are usually more implicit. Consider now another form of implicit agreement, the one between lawmakers and the public.

5.3. Political Agreements

At the risk of glossing over some important features of the relationship, we may say that in a functional democracy a political agreement exists when a politician makes certain representations, and voters give their votes based on those representations. The offer and acceptance of this "promise" then confers an obligation for the politician to follow through and plow the roads, lower taxes, promote family values, or whatever. Note that unlike legal contracts, even when promises are kept, there are often losers. If a politician keeps her promise to reduce military spending, the defense industry loses jobs. But while it would seem that the mistrust of major institutions in general, and the polity in particular, suggests that the public does not believe that politicians act with integrity, the matter may not be so simple.

The issue is sometimes framed as in whose interests legislators vote—their constituents' or their own? If a legislator intentionally misrepresents her actions by accepting an unethical (or illegal) perk in return for a vote favoring some interest group, then there has been a clear violation of the basic conditions of integrity.[13] A more interesting case, one that has recently got a lot of

13. Such matters are the target of the public choice literature. The idea is that interest groups may engage in rent-seeking behavior (offering perks) in order to influence politicians to vote in favor of their specific interests. For instance, a military arms vendor may share the profits from a successful bid with legislators who support their contract. The public choice literature says that this kind of behavior exists because politicians are self-interested like everyone else and also because there is an information problem in the sense that the public and other legal branches do not know about those kinds of deals.

attention in the literature, involves the role of legislator ideology. An ideology is a body of ideas that, when taken together, constitute a program (e.g., neoclassical economics, liberalism). The question we really want to ask is, do legislators deviate from their constituents' interests because of their own ideology, or rather do they faithfully follow their constituents' interests because the political process assures that their ideologies coincide?[14] So long as a political promise has been made, in the former case ideology has contributed to an integrity violation; in the latter case ideology has contributed to political integrity.

The evidence suggests that ideology does indeed affect legislator voting.[15] For example, a politician who prefers the traditional libertarian ideology prefers to vote against any government spending measures that are not consistent with the minimal government functions of protecting individual liberties and property rights. If such a politician votes against a pork barrel government spending bill, can it also be said that she is shirking? Shirking in this context means to act against the interests of the constituents to whom the politician purportedly represents. So the first question to address is, does ideology induce or inhibit shirking?[16]

If the ideological politician purposely acts against her constituents' interests in order to satisfy her own ideological tastes, then ideology causes shirking. If the politician does shirk, she can be thought of as consuming an ideological consumption good. On this account, an ideological politician is more likely to shirk if the cost of consuming an ideological consumption good is low. Costs will be lower the less constituents know and/or care about the shirking.[17] A local politician may be forgiven for not fighting for federal dollars to repaint crosswalks, for instance. On the other hand, for those issues that constituents care about, and thus spend the time and effort to determine

14. In contrast, some authors in Jane Mansbridge's (1990) collection offer cases where politicians act against their own interests in favor of the common good. For instance, Quirk (1990) argues that the deregulation episode from the mid-1970s to the early 1980s was an example of legislators acting against their predicted interests. Keohane (1990) argues that sometimes international politics stems from empathy rather than self-interest. The Marshall Plan might be one example.

15. See, for instance, Poole and Rosenthal 1996.

16. Kalt and Zupan 1984 is the seminal contribution that introduces shirking as an ideological consumption good. See Bender and Lott 1996 for the argument of how ideology and sorting in the political "market" can inhibit political shirking.

17. It should be pointed out that the relevant constituency may not be solely geographical. Instead, it could be that group of voters that could swing an election. Moreover, a candidate also has to worry about satisfying party leaders if she wants to get party support. In some instances the penalty for voting against the party line extends beyond the consequences to the legislator herself. As Longley (2003) reports, in Canadian parliamentary tradition if the members of the ruling party fail to support the prime minister's agenda, parliament is dissolved and a general election is called.

their representative's vote, punishment can be severe. Therefore, ideological politicians may not consume ideological consumption goods if the costs are high, for example, if reelection chances are significantly affected.

An opposing idea suggests that ideology could constrain politician shirking. In a well-functioning political market, voters would know a lot about each politician's views (at least absent preference falsification). Political campaigns provide relevant information about both a candidate's stated positions and past voting records. Therefore, the political process should be able to match ideological candidates with constituents who favor that same ideology. Candidates favoring a conservative ideology have a good chance of prevailing in conservative districts, candidates favoring a liberal ideology in liberal ones, and so on. In this way, politicians "sort" to those districts where the majority of constituents share their views. Since ideological politicians were chosen because of their ideology, they cannot be said to shirk when they vote according to that same ideology. In this scenario, ideology limits shirking because the ideological politician has no reason to deviate from her constituents' interests. By indulging her own tastes she also fulfills her constituents' interests.

The empirical literature seems to favor the latter idea.[18] The most compelling piece of evidence comes from the behavior of legislators in their final terms. If ideology was relevant only insofar as it characterized ideological consumption goods, politicians should indulge their tastes for them in their final period of office because they are no longer under the threat of failed reelection bids. However, the evidence suggests that in their final period of office politicians do not change their voting behavior (though they may vote less often—which is another kind of shirking).[19] The finding that a reduction in costs doesn't change voting behavior is inconsistent with the ideological consumption idea. It is consistent with ideological sorting because ideological politicians were already "consuming" according to their favored ideological tastes. This evidence further suggests that politicians often don't need to conceal their ideologies and engage in preference falsification because they are able to sort to those districts with matching political goals.

Adding integrity to this political mix is straightforward. A minimalist conception implies that a politician keeps whatever promises she makes. A politician of integrity would not consume ideological consumption goods if she promised not to. Thus integrity is inconsistent with the ideological shirking notion. In fact the opposite is true, that is, an ideological politician of integrity has reason not to shirk. If a politician of integrity embraces the mini-

18. See Bender and Lott 1996.

19. Also see Poole and Rosenthal 1996.

malist proposition that "lying is wrong," she has reason to fulfill whatever promises she makes. It does not really matter if she bases those promises on an ideology or not. The reason she would not shirk is that she has made a promise, and to willingly violate it (absent some intervening factors to be discussed) would be counter to the accepted truth of the minimalist proposition and thus incoherent. So the addition of integrity also leads to the absence (or reduction) of political shirking, but for a different reason. The fact that politicians of integrity do not lie is not due to their ideological tastes (or lack thereof), but rather because to shirk would be to lie.

If the politician of integrity was also ideological, sorting in political markets means that "ideological politicians of integrity" will be matched with constituents with the same views. In fact, the existence of integrity makes this even more likely. One information problem confronting voters centers on whether a politician will actually act according to her stated ideology or views. If a politician of integrity is also an incumbent or otherwise has a verifiable record of decisions, voters can infer that there is a higher likelihood that the politician will do as she says in the future. The existence of integrity thus allows voters to match their voting preferences more accurately; voters get the politicians they want.[20] At least that's the implication if the political market works correctly.[21]

But sometimes politicians break their promises. For instance, a politician may promise to cut spending during a campaign but then fail to do so after election. What does integrity require? The issues that need consideration here are mutual deceit and intent. Mutual deceit occurs when parties know and accept that the rules of the game include misrepresentations. What we see, however, is that when a politician does not do as she says, constituents become an-

20. The information problem is further reduced if the politician is also an ideologue. The existing literature on political shirking treats ideology as a preference. In contrast, an ideologue is one who takes certain ideas to be true and is committed to them. The perceived truth of those ideas then gives her reasons to act—a link closely akin to the one established for internal reasons in chapter 3. A politician who reveals this provides voters with additional information that would allow voters to further refine their preference match.

21. If, on the other hand, there is some kind of market failure like an entry barrier, then voters match their preferences with the best *available* candidates. An obvious type of entry barrier is the disproportionately high cost that minor party candidates confront that prevents them from becoming known to voters. In the United States, third-party candidates lack the financial means for effective political advertising, and the rules for getting on different ballots often act as a further entry deterrent. Industrial economists are well aware of the entry-deterring effects of advertising in industry. In a similar way, the U.S. political system is characterized by a two-party duopoly, not unlike Coke and Pepsi. Just as it is arguable whether Coke and Pepsi dominate because of entry barriers or because of consumer preferences, it is not clear if the absence of viable Libertarian and Green parties is due to the same.

gry, other politicians pounce, and the media both exposes the transgression and fuels the indignation. Imagine how long a politician would last who uttered: "Yes, I lied to you, intentionally and willfully, because I know that's what you expected!" Therefore, the response to the promise-breaking politician indicates that the context is not one of mutual deceit. The political context contains moral considerations, and thus a politician of integrity is not free to lie to her constituents.

Turning to the issue of intent, consider the politician who promised to lower taxes but then failed to do so. If the candidate never intended to do so once in office, then she is a liar. Lying is a form of coercion because it intentionally attempts to induce another to act or believe differently than they would if they knew the truth. The apt analogy is the case of contractual fraud. There, the court takes a dim view of intent to mislead a contractual partner and slaps the fraudulent party with criminal penalties. Similarly, voters' highest scorn will go to the politician who intentionally misled them.

However, what if a candidate sincerely intends to lower taxes during the campaign but comes to find out that she severely underestimated the costs of doing so after she is elected? In fact, suppose that based on new budget estimates she judges that to follow through on her promise would be immoral because it would either seriously harm the poor and/or shift an unconscionably higher tax burden onto future generations. Now the politician faces a dilemma: whether to break her campaign promise or keep it and cause other, presumably greater harm. In this case there was no intent to lie if the politician tries to minimize harm. The point is not to say which is the correct answer but rather to illustrate that, based on intent, a politician *could* conceivably break her campaign promise and still be considered a person of integrity. A politician who did not intend to break a promise but ends up doing so may suffer political costs, just like a contractual party who breaches and suffers material costs as a result, but need not violate the conditions of integrity. The difference is that in the contractual setting the aggrieved party is compensated for the breach; in the political case aggrieved citizens (those who expected lower taxes) remain harmed (even though others benefit), and the level of trust in both the politician and also the democratic process may fall. Moreover, contractual parties know the rules of the game and expect occasional breaches. Perhaps in the few conceivable instances where the politician's reasoning was sufficiently sound to pass the hypothetical reasonable person criterion mentioned in section 5.1, then these kinds of harms and political costs would be minimal.

Of course one's intent may be difficult to ascertain. One may not even fully recognize one's own intent. The situation is perhaps most problematic in politics because promises are often vague. A promise to lower taxes is reasonably precise, but ones to promote American values or to make America strong are not. A politician may make vague promises or frame intended actions generally because she does not have a precise agenda at the campaign stage. In that case, there need not be intent to deceive. However, if a politician makes vague promises in order to obscure her intent while in office, that in itself is a deception, in which a politician of integrity is not free to indulge. The justification of trying to minimize the consequences of unpopular decisions would rarely, if ever, suffice to pardon misleading intent.[22] As Bok notes, even in matters of national security, the public expects, wants, and deserves the truth, and attempts to conceal actions have failed miserably (e.g., Vietnam). Integrity violations of this kind, and others less momentous, cause direct harm, contribute to the erosion of public trust, and further tempt politicians to engage in the additional deceit of miscalculating the costs and benefits of their actions in order to fulfill their own, not the public's, interests.

This chapter discussed lying in some detail and considered in particular the idea of mutual deceits. Based on the minimalist principle that "lying is wrong," we saw that persons of integrity are not free to commit fraud in legal contexts, though they may breach in some circumstances, while integrity among politicians can help ideological sorting in political markets. Neither context can be said to be characterized by mutual deceit, though promise breaking can sometimes occur with limited consequences. To further develop these ideas, we now consider the important context of the workplace setting.

---

22. McGraw (1998) notes further that politicians often invoke moral reasons for their actions, but that the public is not very good at judging the sincerity of such claims.

Chapter 6

The Employment Agreement

Of all the myriad types of contracts, the employment contract is perhaps most fundamental. Two reasons jump out. First, it underlies the theory of the firm, a topic itself so central because to understand firms is to gain a deep understanding of how markets work. Second, almost everyone but the most or least privileged has worked or will work for wages at some time. The employment relationship is a particularly important relationship for most people, and working often comprises an important element of one's identity. Therefore, the employment agreement provides a logical and important extension of the preceding discussion on contracts.

The employment agreement also provides a stark example of how the addition of integrity leads to a different conclusion than the ones found in the current literatures. Currently, the theory of the firm focuses on the problem of worker shirking (or opportunistic behavior by contractual partners) and ways of mitigating it. That problem is not really relevant for workers of integrity, because to shirk would be to lie—at least if the worker had an explicit agreement with her employer. Based on workers of integrity, the essence of the firm transforms into a problem of how to coordinate different input contributions, particularly knowledge contributions. It turns out, interestingly, that even if firms do optimally promote the conditions necessary for workers to act with integrity, that by itself would be insufficient to promote the knowledge contributions associated with innovation in firms. Moreover, absent those optimal conditions, mutual deceit could be a problem. So the implication is that by promoting clear and fair agreements firms not only minimize the possibility of mutual deceit, they also indirectly create the conditions necessary for innovation that induce workers to act on other motivations.

To shed light on these issues, I first briefly summarize the literature on the theory of the firm and highlight the assumption of worker shirking/opportunism. (Opportunism generally refers to self-interested behavior in contracts, while shirking refers to the same in the employment context; for the discussion that follows, I use the terms interchangeably.) Next, I address the notion of workers of integrity and the important issue of mutual deceit. How workers of integrity could be managed follows, with a focus on the role of knowledge in organizations. The chapter closes with a discussion of how integrity could fit into the view of the firm in other disciplines, and a few final thoughts.

6.1. The Theory of the Firm and the Importance of Shirking

In economics, the big questions in the theory of the firm center on why firms exist, how they are internally organized, and what they produce. The first question is fundamental for economics because economists usually believe that markets, characterized by price-mediated exchanges, are the most efficient way to allocate resources. But, in some sense, firms seem to question the efficacy of markets. The second question about the way firms are organized refers to issues like the extent of hierarchy and who controls the decision-making processes. Most business firms are organized such that the owners of capital (or their agents), rather than workers, make the major decisions. The question is, why?[1] The last question refers to the boundaries of the firm's activities. Some firms operate in a vast array of markets; most do not. This line of research asks questions like, why doesn't an airline company make its own airplanes, or go into the computer hardware business?

The undisputed father of the theory of the firm in economics is Ronald Coase. In his seminal 1937 article entitled "The Nature of the Firm," he asked the most fundamental question of all: why do firms even exist? His key insight was that spot-exchange markets are costly, and in the case of a capital owner who seeks to hire the varied input contributions of many workers, one contract, the employee agreement, could substitute for the innumerable transactions that would otherwise be necessary. Firms are born in order to minimize the transaction costs associated with the market, in particular the costs associated with discovering relevant prices and the negotiation of the various tasks required for any given activity. The employment agreement, the essence of the firm, gives the employer the right to direct employees' activities in return for wages and benefits, subject only to whatever conditions are bargained for and any legal proscriptions. Coase also tackled the boundary question by

1. This question is of particular interest to advocates of the labor-managed firm (and worker participation in general). A vast literature addresses the issue; see Dow 2003.

positing that firms will continue to internalize activities until the cost of doing so, for instance, the cost of added bureaucracy, just exceeds the cost of acquiring the activity in the market (from another firm, say). An airline doesn't make its own airplanes because it can acquire them more cheaply from outside sources.

This transaction cost approach has been refined and redirected by more recent authors who have come to emphasize the hazards of reliance expenditures in contracts.[2] If one party invests in what's called "specific assets," assets that lose their value outside of the contractual relationship, and if the contract is only imperfectly enforceable, then it may be advantageous for one party to simply buy out the assets and skills of the other (i.e., integrate) rather than face the potential risks of contractual breach. Real-life contracts are not perfectly enforceable because, first, contractual parties cannot costlessly incorporate all future contingencies into a contract and, second, because it is costly to use courts (which can make mistakes). The hazard becomes central because it is assumed that contractual parties will act "opportunistically," strategically, and self-interestedly.[3] This contemporary version of transaction cost theory especially focuses on the boundaries of the firm, but also its internal organization because those with the most to lose from opportunistic behavior are assumed to be the ones who will obtain decision-making rights.

The other major theory of the firm is the agency approach. That approach can be further differentiated into its positive and formal variants. The seminal positive agency articles focus on monitoring in the firm.[4] The idea is that the classical firm is characterized by a central monitor who is party to all contracts, can alter the membership of the firm, and who is the residual-

2. The seminal references are Klein, Crawford, and Alchian 1978; Williamson 1985; Grossman and Hart 1986.

3. To illustrate, suppose that an automobile manufacturer needs tires, compares the costs of making versus buying, and, absent contractual hazards, figures that it is cheaper to buy them. The problem is that once it decides on one tire supplier from all the possibilities, it has to enter a long-term contract. Once the contract is executed, the manufacturer is likely to incur costs peculiar to the relationship, like locating a manufacturing plant close to the tire producer, for instance. Once the manufacturing plant is located close to the tire producer the tire producer gains ex post bargaining power because the cost of bringing in an outside tire producer should the relationship sour increases (assuming location is important; also note that the tire producer may confront contractual hazards if the location increases the cost of selling to other buyers). Since the tire producer knows this, it can extract concessions from the manufacturer. The manufacturer would have to concede if it estimates the costs of prevailing in court as being too high. Knowing all of this at the onset could induce the manufacturer to just buy out the tire producer in the first place because then all contractual hazards would be eliminated. Bureaucratic costs of monitoring tire production in-house would increase, however. The make-buy decision involves a comparison of the lowered cost from the reduction of contractual hazards with the increased costs of added bureaucracy.

4. Alchian and Demsetz 1972; Jensen and Meckling 1976.

claimant (gets the profits). The key assumption is that the technology of production is such that team members (say, in a partnership) working collectively can produce more than if they each worked individually and independently. The problem is that if an outside contractor paying for the team's services based that payment on output, then each member could benefit by shirking by sharing the cost of that shirking with the other team members. Therefore, each member has incentive to shirk. Moreover, even if she cared, the outside contractor could not infer how hard each was working just by observing output because of the team technology assumption. Given this scenario, workers will eschew partnership forms of organization, at least in most conditions, and favor the classical firm where the central monitor can track each individual's *contributions* and pay them accordingly. In the classical firm workers are monitored and paid according to their marginal product, and the central monitor's incentive to provide this service well is guaranteed by virtue of her status as residual-claimant. In the corporate firm, managers (or owner-managers) are prevented from shirking or perk-taking by stockholder monitoring.

The formal agency or principal-agent literature focuses on constructing optimal incentive contracts in the face of uncertainty.[5] The context is one where a principal contracts with an agent to act on her behalf. For instance, the principal could be an employer contracting with an employee (the agent) to provide effort of one sort or another in return for compensation. The problem is that there is some kind of uncertainty over production possibilities or maybe demand that prevents the employer from inferring the employee's actions just by observing the outcome of those actions. Did the employee produce only a small amount (which is observed) because of low effort (unobserved) or because of some production difficulty (also unobserved)? Or, did the fast-food franchisee have good sales some month because of hard work or because of high demand for the franchiser's product? Since the principal cannot infer the agent's action by observing the outcome, the agent could misrepresent the real reason for observed outcomes. The principal's problem, then, is to figure out a way to get the agent to provide high effort regardless of the environment. One possible way of doing that is to just offer the agent a contract in which the agent is compensated according to output. The problem with that kind of contract, at least from the agent's perspective, is that it requires the agent to take on all of the risk. Assuming that agents are risk averse, that kind of contract, by itself, is unattractive. It turns out that the contracts with the best incentive properties also have the worst risk proper-

5. See, for instance, Holmstrom 1982; Hart and Holmstrom 1987; Sappington 1991.

ties, and vice versa.[6] To overcome this problem, optimal incentive contracts, which can be mathematically very complicated, incorporate information about observable elements in the environment. Observations about an agent's peers, for instance, may be used to infer something about the environment the agent is operating in. If an employee's co-workers are producing a lot, that tells the employer something about the environment. That kind of signal can be used in writing an optimal incentive contract in the first place.

Capabilities theory, which is a lesser-known approach but popular in the business literature, has been making headway in economics. This theory emphasizes the pooled knowledge and skills inherent in firms.[7] Capabilities refer to what a firm can do. In this literature, a firm is characterized by habits, routines, its own history, and its knowledge and capabilities, much of which are institutional rather than personal. Since the basic idea is that the firm is a repository of pooled knowledge and skills, the focus is on knowledge and production rather than exchange, and a crucial element is that firm decision makers must act under structural uncertainty—the type of uncertainty that does not allow decision makers to specify all the alternatives ex ante. Furthermore, because of the tacit nature of knowledge, a firm is capable of doing things that it cannot easily describe. Together these elements suggest that it is futile for either firms or economists to try to prespecify actual production functions. Instead, the focus is placed on enhancing capabilities, coordinating different contributions, and the performance of various organizational structures in different economic environments. I will return to this view of the firm later in the chapter.

What is most notable about the contemporary transaction cost and agency variants of the theory of the firm is their basic starting point about agent (worker or contractor) behavior. Borrowing from utility theory, the agent is characterized as instrumentally rational. But additionally, one relevant preference is assumed, namely, that workers favor leisure over effort. That means workers will shirk if they could get away with it regardless of what they said or agreed to. In this way, opportunism or shirking becomes the central problem of the firm. Any other kind of representations by workers against working is seen as cheap talk or hot air; they are not credible because they misrepresent the agent's true preference—leisure over effort. That means, of course, that a disposition against lying (e.g., emanating from preference-in-

6. Fixed wage contracts, where the employer pays an agreed amount no matter the outcome, have great risk-indemnifying features for the employee but bad incentive properties from the employer's point of view because the employee gets the same wage whether she provides low or high effort.
7. See, for example, Teece 1980, 1982; Nelson and Winter 1982; Lazonick 1990; Prahalad and Hamel 1990; Kogut and Zander 1992, 1996; Langlois 1992; Minkler 1993a, 1993b; Loasby 1998.

tegrity or commitment-integrity) is not considered. The usual reason given is methodological simplicity. Oliver Williamson, a main proponent of contemporary transaction cost theory, embraces this view despite his acknowledgment that "people usually will do what they say (and some will do more) without self-consciously asking whether the effort is justified by expected discounted net gains."[8] In contrast, it could be said that *the modern theory of the firm is based on a lie.*[9]

6.2. Worker Integrity

The primary implication of integrity by firm members is as simple as it is profound. If firm members embrace the minimalist principle of not lying, then once agreements have been struck specifying each party's obligations and entitlements, the firm can go about the business of fulfilling its mission. If everyone, principals and agents, could be counted on as being persons of integrity, the firm would not have to worry about expending significant resources on monitoring and other effort-assuring strategies, and could instead focus its attention on coordinating resources most expeditiously. Workers, too, would not have to worry about the firm reneging on its promises, implicit or explicit, of good working conditions, promises for advancement, and the like. If both sides of the employment contract could be counted on as being persons of integrity, the firm would be characterized by trust. Something more would be needed to assure innovation in firms, but if everyone was characterized by integrity, the contemporary transaction cost and agency theories of the firm would be nothing more than interesting intellectual exercises.

Of course not everyone is characterized by integrity, just as not everyone can be characterized as an opportunistic shirker. To what extent then does integrity exist in firms? Moreover, and relatedly, how big of a problem is shirking in firms? I now turn to those important questions.

It turns out that there are three problems with solely relying on the incentive assumption to characterize opportunism and shirking. First, little evidence exists to support it; none exists for work in team settings.[10] Second,

8. Williamson 1996, 49.

9. See Hodgson 2004 for one attempt that argues there is more to the firm than opportunism or shirking.

10. Prendergast (1999) provides the most comprehensive literature review of the underlying assumptions of agency theory, including the incentive one. He does find limited support for the incentive assumption in "simple jobs," those that do not exhibit a team nature or necessitate joint contributions from different members. Piecework payment schemes can boost salaries and productivity in windshield installation, Canadian tree planting, and, on an aggregate level, Chinese

and again contrary to the agency literature, the vast majority of employers do not use pay-for-performance incentive schemes, instead opting for subjective performance evaluations to determine pay, promotion, and training.[11] If shirking was the universal problem economists assume, we would expect to see more incentive mechanisms in real life of the sort predicted by the literature. Finally, there is evidence for alternative motivations. There is overwhelming experimental evidence suggesting that people do not always act on instrumental rationality as usually conceived, as noted in chapter 1. There is also evidence for moral motivations of the sort emanating from integrity, intrinsic motivation, fairness considerations, and peer pressure. The existence of any combination of these alternative motivations could prevent shirking, even in the absence of incentive alignment based on opportunistic behavior.

For example, to address these issues directly I commissioned an extensive national survey to find out about individuals' attitudes (and their determinants) toward shirking.[12] To start, the following question was posed.

> Suppose that it is almost impossible for your employer to check up on you. Would you say that you are very likely, somewhat likely, somewhat unlikely, or very unlikely to work hard if you agreed to?

In response to that question, 82.7 percent responded "very likely," 12.1 percent "somewhat likely," 1.9 percent "somewhat unlikely," and 1.6 percent "very unlikely." Surveyors sometimes group the first two and last two categories, resulting in 94.8 percent of the respondents claiming that they are likely to work hard, *if they agreed to,* and 3.5 percent claiming otherwise (the remaining 1.7 percent either did not know or did not answer). So long as an employment

---

agriculture. Nagin et al. (2002) analyze data from a telephone soliciting firm and find that solicitor performance does decline for some members when monitoring declines. However, they also find that a substantial fraction are disinclined to shirk, and they suggest that managers need to balance monitoring and incentives against fairness considerations. Again, their data cover a work setting where joint contributions are unnecessary. In contrast, Shanteau and Harrison (1991) conducted a series of experiments to test the commitments of subjects of an ex ante employment contract and find that breach based on incentives only occurred for significant numbers after extensive cuing by the researchers.

11. See Prendergast 1999; Macleod and Parent 1999; Ichniowski and Shaw 2003. The exception seems to be for sales and machinist workers.

12. Minkler 2004. Studies of this sort have to carefully address measurement error, especially that stemming from social desirability bias. How do we know that respondents answered truthfully? To address this concern, many controls were used. In order to maximize the possibility of truthful responses, the survey was scrutinized by focus groups and professional survey researchers, and was pretested. Since remaining social desirability bias could be correlated with the demographic characteristics of respondents, six demographic variables were included in the regression analysis. The results reported include all of these controls.

agreement is in place, an important caveat that is the topic of the next section, the evidence in this survey is consistent with the others that suggest that shirking in firms is not a big problem. So why would individuals not shirk?

To answer that question, respondents were asked to rank alternatives on a 0 to 10 scale. The following gives the question and alternatives (from highest to lowest ranked), along with mean scores in parentheses.

> Now we want to ask why you would be likely to work hard. On a scale of 0–10, with 0 being not important at all, and 10 being very important, how important is each of the following in determining why it is likely you would work hard?
>
> 1. It is the morally right thing to do. (9.10)
> 2. I enjoy my work. (8.59)
> 3. I wouldn't want to let down my coworkers or get them mad at me. (6.95)
> 4. I may get a raise or promotion if I do a good job. (6.69)
> 5. My employer might catch me. (3.08)
> 6. My employer has convinced me to feel guilty if I don't work hard. (2.37)

Note that the top-ranking alternative is consistent with the moral motivation of workers of integrity. To break an employment agreement is to lie, and apparently many judge that to be wrong. The second captures the notion of intrinsic motivation, or the enjoyment some get just by doing a good job. They don't shirk because doing interesting work has value and provides more utility than consuming leisure.[13] Importantly, these first two alternatives are also significant in regression analyses that look at the variation in the different categories of the propensity to shirk. The third alternative captures peer pressure, or the notion that a worker cares about her co-workers. In that case, the worker may succumb to workplace norms (e.g., to work hard) in order not to feel the sting of social sanctions, like ostracism and barely veiled negative gossip.[14] The fourth refers to positive incentives, while the last two, meant to capture negative incentives (e.g., monitoring and firm pressure) were judged unimportant by respondents.

13. Interestingly, the evidence suggests that some of the very strategies recommended by economists—monitoring and pay-for-performance payment schemes—might act to crowd out intrinsic motivation and decrease effort. The reason is that those strategies redirect the locus of control of the agent's contributions from the agent to the principal. That loss of control or of autonomy causes the crowding-out. See Frey 1997b; Frey and Jegen 2001.

14. See Kandel and Lazear 1992; Fehr and Gächter 2000a.

Employees also care about fairness. Fairness in firms usually refers to the reciprocal aspect of relationships. If an employer uses fair processes to mete out tasks and rewards, and if the outcomes are perceived as fair, employees might reciprocate by providing effort.[15] To capture this idea, the following three questions were asked (with the mean response in parentheses).

> On a scale of 0–10, with 0 being very dishonest and 10 being very honest, how honest would you say today's employers are? (5.94)
>
> On a scale of 0–10, with 0 being very dishonest and 10 being very honest, how important is it that your employer be honest? (9.62)
>
> On a scale of 0–10, with 0 being not very likely at all and 10 being very likely, how likely is it that you would keep an agreement to do a good job if you know your employer to be honest? (9.69)

While workers do not judge employers to be overwhelmingly honest, they do indicate a willingness to keep agreements with honest employers. The degree to which a firm is perceived as fair might also play an important indirect role in an employee's willingness to keep agreements, as will be discussed in the next section.

So shirking may not be the problem most economists think, and for reasons not usually considered. Workers may not shirk because of other motives. While intrinsic, fairness, and peer-pressure motivations have started to emerge in the literature, the notion of worker integrity has been completely absent. But workers of integrity could also be expected to work hard, and it doesn't require a heroic leap of faith to believe that many in today's work force are guided by the minimalist moral principle. In order for integrity to matter, however, there must be an employment agreement, and employees must know the rules of the game and consent to them. Could a worker who has agreed to work hard still shirk and be considered a person of integrity? The answer hinges on the issues of mutual deceit, moral standing, and their relationship to fairness.

6.3. Mutual Deceit in the Employment Agreement

If all parties in the firm knew about and accepted misrepresentations, then persons of integrity could lie freely without effect. The old Soviet adage "we

15. See Cohen-Charash and Spector 2001; Fehr and Falk 2002.

pretend to work, they pretend to pay us" characterizes such workplace environments. At first blush, the problem may seem analogous to the one described by economists, that is, where firms are characterized by cheap talk, and the real problem is incentive alignment. Yet it is not because the solutions are different. To solve the central problem of the firm, shirking, economists recommend monitoring, incentive contracts, and the like. In the case of workers of integrity where mutual deceit is the problem, the solution is to get the parties to understand their true moral obligations. That key distinction differentiates analyses that assume workers are instrumentally rational versus the one here that assumes workers identify with the minimalist moral principle of "lying is wrong."

The solution to mutual deceit, in turn, may depend to a large extent on the moral standing of other parties. Suppose that an agreement has been struck between a principal and agent, and that each believes that the specified obligations carry moral weight. If the principal violates her obligation to provide a good working environment, for example, is the agent still obligated to keep her promise to work hard? As discussed in the previous chapter, that question would be the same as asking if it is ever justified to lie to liars. Kant says no, but based on Bok's normative criteria the answer is yes if it prevents harm and there are no other alternatives. The answer is no otherwise. Still, as a positive descriptive matter, others may employ an even lower standard, one based on the perceived moral standing of the liar. Based on some kind of notion of reciprocal fairness, some will believe that once another has lied they are no longer entitled to the truth.

So if an employer lies to a worker who otherwise has reason to work hard, three options emerge. First, the worker could believe the principle of lying to be inviolable, at least in normal workplace settings. Such a person would continue to keep her promise, at least until she found another job (or found a way to teach the employer to tell the truth). Second, the worker could take the employer's lie as evidence that the relationship had changed to one of mutual deceit and thus she was no longer obligated to keep her own promise to work hard. If true, the worker could still be characterized as a person of integrity. The problem of course is that if tempted (perhaps subconsciously) by self-deceit the worker could fictitiously characterize the relationship as one of mutual deceit even when the employer did not. The employee could even perceptually skew evidence to fit the account of a lie and a change to mutual deceit. But in the case where the employer does *not* accept a change in the rules of the game, in order for the worker to remain a person of integrity, she must use a lower standard for when it is acceptable to lie. So, third, a worker of integrity could violate her own promise if she no longer attributes moral standing to her employer. That is, the worker still believes she is obligated to not lie, but only with those who are entitled to the obligation. By lying, the employer has forfeited that entitlement. As a positive matter, some workers will surely use the reasoning of this third case. Normatively, it is more problematic for the reasons given by Sissela Bok and as discussed in the previous chapter. Since lying harms society (diminished trust), the lied to (coercion), and the liar herself (character blow), it can only be morally justified if it prevents a greater harm, and even cases satisfying that strict criterion are rarely justified.

Analogously, the employer could intend to keep her promises but find herself with a bunch of lying, shirking workers as described by economists. Her options would be similar to those just mentioned. So the question really becomes how to assure that all parties have reason to act on their principles, especially the minimalist one. A clear solution is to make sure that workplace agreements exist. Absent agreement, no violations could occur. To be sure, agents may provide effort for other reasons like positive incentives or intrinsic motivations, but without agreements integrity is not operative.

In the survey mentioned earlier, 66.1 percent thought that such agreements existed in the workplace and were important to honor, while 19.7 percent thought no such agreements existed.[16] The latter group represents a real missed opportunity to bind employers and employees together in mutually beneficial ways, mediated by principled behavior. Another group thought that workplace agreements existed but were not important to honor; they registered 11.3 percent of the responses. That group represents those who view the firm either as a context of mutual deceit or as peopled with those who lack moral standing. Given these concerns, once agreements are made, the next issue is how to assure that mutual deceit and the lack of moral standing do not undermine their force. That issue turns pivotally on the role of fairness.

Economists typically invoke reciprocity, real or anticipated, for their notions of fairness.[17] In contrast, those working in psychology and social psychology have identified three different types of fairness (sometimes referred to as "justice"): distributive, procedural, and interactional.[18] The first focuses on the perceived fairness of outcomes (e.g., income and promotion distribution in organizations). Perceived unfair outcomes are expected to affect a person's emotions (e.g., anger) and cognitions, which in turn affect their behavior. Procedural fairness, in contrast, focuses on the perceived fairness of the

16. Minkler 2004.

17. For instance, see Rabin 1993.

18. Cohen-Charash and Spector 2001.

process determining outcomes. A fair process is consistent, unbiased, accurate, prone to corrections, inclusive, and ethical. The last, interactional fairness, refers to the perceived fairness of interpersonal interactions by particularly focusing on polite, honest, and respectful communications.[19]

All types of fairness—distributive, procedural, and interactional—sincerely exhibited by another contributes to a person's moral standing. It is a cognitive problem to recognize these traits, not a social one.[20] Thus where sincere fairness occurs, mutual deceit and the absence of moral standing rationally do not. Therefore, one very real way for firms to assure that workers of integrity have reason to act on their principles is to act fairly. Note that fairness considerations play an indirect role in this account because they signal intentions regarding the rules of the game and also confirm the moral standing of one to the other.[21]

Evidence documents the relationship between fairness and worker behavior. In their 2001 meta-analysis, Yochi Cohen-Charash and Paul Spector study the correlates of distributive, procedural, and interactional types of fairness from 190 laboratory and field studies consisting of 64,757 participants. The evidence suggests that each type of fairness is conceptually distinct, but also that each is highly correlated with the others. A key result finds that work performance is mainly related to perceived procedural fairness (mean correlation coefficient of .47 for 11 field studies with 2,061 participants). Performance included measures of effort, official performance ratings, in-role behavior ratings, and study-specific performance measures. Similarly, perceptions of distributive and procedural fairness are negatively related to counterproductive work behaviors (mean correlation coefficients of .24 and .29, respectively, for 3 field studies with 597 participants). This evidence is consistent with the view that fair employers attain a certain moral standing with their workers.

Now consider further what a firm can expect if it has agreements with workers of integrity.

19. Interactional fairness might be closely related to the reciprocity notions found in economics. Examples of those most closely aligned with distributive fairness might include Konow's (1996) focus on allocations varying in proportion to one's contribution and Fehr and Schmidt's (1999) focus on inequity aversion. Examples related to procedural fairness include not exploiting fortuitous circumstances (Kahneman, Knetsch, and Thaler 1986) and equal division of gifts (Frey and Bohnet 1995).

20. Landy and Becker 1987.

21. Most accounts of fairness are more direct. That is, I may provide something of value to you because you provided something of value to me.

6.4. Managing Workers of Integrity

If workers could be counted on to be persons of integrity, what implications emerge for the firm, particularly its managers?[22] To answer that question, we have to know a little more about the roles and functions of a manager. For much of the contemporary transaction cost and agency literature, the manager's chief function is to monitor workers or to otherwise construct incentive alignment systems to assure effort (prevent shirking). For the capabilities literature the issue is more about coordinating various input contributions in the most expeditious way. That literature focuses on the management of knowledge.

To possess information about something is to possess facts or data. In contrast, to know or possess knowledge about something is to understand it. Knowledge requires a theory of the system that is capable of explicating facts or data.[23] Moreover, knowledge is empirical, potentially tacit, and often the source of "surprises." Knowledge is empirical because, as famously described by Friedrich Hayek, those seeking it search for "knowledge of particular circumstances of time and place."[24] The empirical nature of knowledge suggests that it is contextual and fleeting. Knowledge is tacit if it can't be communicated or transferred to other individuals. The details of skillful performances are often difficult to articulate to another.[25] Finally, knowledge often stems from "surprises," unanticipated events not originally planned or intended. New ideas are surprises in this sense. Interestingly, ideas are nondeterministic in the same way that the choice of principles is nondeterministic in conscious reflection—the basis for individual autonomy and integrity in the first place.

Given the nature of knowledge, what's involved in coordinating it? Two primary issues stand out. First, knowledge has to be transferred smoothly, meaning that knowledge contributions have to be coherently passed on to the second stage of production. Second, it has to be created, augmented, and expanded.[26] Knowledge is created through the addition of new ideas, the very origin of innovation. Management has to figure out how to assure both of these functions. But once management practices and culture have been implemented, they become what has been called "firm-specific pool resources,"

22. This section is adapted from Minkler 2003.
23. Minkler 1993a; also see O'Driscoll and Rizzo 1985.
24. Hayek 1945, 102.
25. Nelson and Winter 1982, 73.
26. Kogut and Zander (1996) make a similar distinction and suggest that firms are social communities that create the "discourse and learning that promote innovation and promoted behavior."

or common organizational rules and routines.[27] On this view, a social dilemma arises whereby firm members may choose to free ride on these resources to the detriment of the organization as a whole, which is analogous to shirking in the sense that free riders benefit from the efforts of others without having to undergo the costs of contributing their own effort. An example of such behavior would be the violation of accepted procedures for doing work tasks, which, since they are interrelated, means that others have to decode the nonconforming processes, which in turn could slow down the transmission of knowledge. Free riding on the creation of knowledge just means that the offender benefits from the ideas of others, perhaps because the latter assures the firm's competitive edge and hence its continued existence as a place of employment. A free rider doesn't have to go through the effort of being the source of new ideas herself.[28]

Managers, therefore, confront three kinds of performance problems, beginning with the shirking problem so ubiquitous in the prominent economic theories of the firm. The second, somewhat analogous problem, relates to the free riding on the transfer of knowledge. The third involves free riding on the creation of knowledge. In reality, management practices recognize that there are several classes of motivations, including self-interest, adherence to moral principles, intrinsic motivations, peer pressure, and fairness considerations. For the purposes of the present discussion, we confine the focus to the role of integrity for those workers who could be so characterized. What kinds of problems could management practices be expected to solve when aimed at those of integrity?

If workers are persons of integrity, then both these problems—shirking and free riding on the transfer of knowledge—could be solved with management practices establishing agreements that specify provisions on effort and knowledge-transfer obligations in clear language. Clear agreements ensure that workers know what is expected. Much of what appears to be shirking may be the result of misaligned expectations. If effort and knowledge-transfer requirements can be specified in a detailed manner, that problem is solved. Workers must also be given to understand that their obligations carry moral

---

27. Osterloh, Frost, and Frey 2002.

28. It turns out that free riding in the creation of knowledge is not analogous to shirking because shirking presumes that a principal could direct the correct effort if he could observe it (and the relevant variables). A principal could not direct the creation of specific ideas because they are surprises to the agent and thus the principal as well. This information/knowledge distinction lies behind the criticism that the agency theory of the firm misses a most prominent feature of firms. See Minkler 1993a.

force. That means that they must believe that the workplace context is not one of mutual deceit, and that the other parties to the agreement possess moral standing. As suggested earlier, one way, perhaps the best one, to do that is for management to institute practices that are fair in both process and outcome. For these two types of problems then, clear agreements and fair practices substitute for monitoring and incentive contracts. Once again, the existence of integrity clearly distinguishes these recommended types of management practices from the ones offered in contemporary transaction cost and agency literatures.

The existence of integrity is of less help in solving the idea-creation problem. In order for integrity to be a factor there would have to be some kind of moral obligation that could be exacted on the creation of ideas. Certainly "not lying" is insufficient. Since an idea is a deep expression of a state of mind, the most intimate aspect of the self, no universal moral principle can obligate us to surrender it to another. Philosopher Annette Baier frames it this way: "We are under no permanent duty to deliver the truth about our states of mind to others, and it would be an intolerably inquisition-prone society that would force us to take on such a duty, say by a promise."[29] Such obligations would induce people to conceal their private thoughts in order to prevent intimate intrusion, and the whole institution of promise keeping would be degraded.[30] Thus, even if a clear agreement could be executed (how could it specify particular "surprise" contributions?), there would be no moral obligation to perform. To address this problem, management may instead consider practices that bear on intrinsic motivations (e.g., interesting work), self-interest (e.g., positive incentives like profit-sharing and rank-order tournaments), and perhaps the direct, as opposed to indirect, effects of fairness motivations.[31] In fact, fair agreements can help provide the conditions necessary for workers to act on their intrinsic motivations, thereby indirectly promoting the conditions necessary for knowledge creation. So while management practices that give workers of integrity reason to keep their agreements will facilitate the smooth functioning of a firm's capabilities, additional measures are needed to assure the creation of new ideas.

29. Baier 1990, 272.

30. The issue is analogous to preference falsification, which no kind of legislation can overcome.

31. That practices like profit sharing could induce ideas is not to concede that agency theory is correct on this issue. The problems addressed by agency theory could all be solved if the principal could observe what the agent observes. The theory does not address agent ideas. It just so happens that practices like profit sharing could elicit agent ideas if the agent was motivated by self-interest. Minkler 1993b analyzes that issue at length.

6.5. Integrity and Other Views of the Firm

Not only have organization theorists in psychology and management been major contributors to the capabilities theory of the firm, but they also focus on different aspects of organizations than is typical for economists.

Focusing on the creation and coordination of knowledge, one strand of the capabilities view of the firm also emphasizes the social nature of motivation and knowledge. For instance, Bruce Kogut and Udo Zander argue that employment constitutes a very important component of individual identity.[32] People tend to closely identify with their employer and community of co-workers. That identification shapes the values and rules one adheres to, as well as the discourse and coordination of knowledge. A social identity can promote cooperation and a smoother coordination of knowledge than if self-interest was the sole motivation. However, social identity also creates insiders and outsiders. If outsiders are excluded from the discourse and coordination of knowledge, as they almost certainly will be, certain capabilities will not be available to the firm. So despite the fact that social identity promotes productive relationships among included members, it nevertheless limits the boundaries of firms by excluding those who might otherwise contribute.

In a similar vein, others suggest that a central problem for firms is to manage knowledge with social dilemma characteristics, that is, knowledge created and transferred that benefits everyone, but in which there exist incentives to free ride.[33] A cooperative corporate culture and common organizational rules are examples of knowledge that can be undersupplied if they can be consumed freely but are costly to contribute to and provide. One way firms can assure the provision of this kind of social knowledge is to provide a work environment that acts on members' intrinsic motivation. Members will contribute if their work is interesting and if they have some measure of control over their own contributions. Furthermore, the notion of crowding-out suggests that workers may even withhold contributions if the employer uses a reward system based on incentives if they view the locus of control being shifted from their grasp. So for firms for which social knowledge is important, a profitable strategy may be to encourage participation, cooperative interactions, and personal relationship building.

As I have already noted, the idea of workers of integrity is largely consistent with the capabilities view of the firm; it is also consistent with the contri-

32. Kogut and Zander 1996. Also see Akerlof and Kranston 2005 for a more recent attempt to model worker identity.
33. Osterloh, Frost, and Frey 2002.

butions just discussed. It is reasonable to infer that a worker of integrity is also a social being, and as such she forms an important part of her identity from her work relationships. Moreover, a worker of integrity not only identifies with her social community but also necessarily with moral principles. Adding the notion of integrity into the analyses that focus on the social nature of knowledge and motivation would simply mean an additional emphasis on clear and fair agreements in firms. Such agreements would help assure that workers have reason to act on the minimalist moral principle, which would facilitate trust and cooperative relationships among the firm's diverse contributors.

Another branch of organization theory explicitly addresses the psychological considerations of contracting. This approach, perhaps most closely associated with Denise Rousseau, maintains that all organizations use contracts, implicitly if not explicitly.[34] A psychological contract "refers to an individual's beliefs regarding terms and conditions of a reciprocal exchange agreement between that person and another party."[35] Since contract terms are often difficult or impossible to explicitly specify, and because even explicit terms invite subjective interpretation, performance depends on beliefs and expectations about promises. Beliefs and expectations can be most closely aligned when contracts cover simple exchanges, are clear, and are explicitly agreed upon by all parties.[36] When relationships are more long term and open ended, and involve contributions, support, and rewards that are more difficult to explicitly specify, the possibility of a misalignment between each party's beliefs and expectations increases.

Firms characterized by contracts with low ambiguity, low commitment, low learning, and low identification are called *transactional*. These are the types of firms most studied by economists. Employers are modeled as wanting high effort for the lowest wage possible, and workers are modeled as wanting a high wage and low effort. The relationship does not involve commitment, trust, or any kind of personal identification. In a sense, worker expectations are easy to manage because they are low; pay is commensurate with well-defined performance standards. Examples include retail clerks hired during the holidays and newly minted graduates hired by large public accounting firms to do standard audit and tax preparations (who usually only stay for a short time in order to take the CPA exam and wait for a more permanent position elsewhere).

In contrast, contracts characterized by high commitment and identifi-

34. See especially Rousseau and Parks 1993; Rousseau 1995.

35. Rousseau and Parks 1993, 19.

36. Rousseau (1995, 9–10) calls shared psychological contracts among a social group *normative contracts*.

cation, and open-ended terms are called *relational* if terms are difficult to specify or are ambiguous, and *balanced* if performance terms can be well specified.[37] In these kinds of firms workers are expected to make contributions beyond the effort versus leisure decision, much like in the capabilities view of the firm, and employers are expected to provide ongoing support, loyalty, and advancement opportunities, as well as good compensation. Relational contracts can be found in family and small businesses and corporations. Balanced contracts characterize the high-involvement teams found in corporations of all sizes.

Since psychological contracts are open to subjective interpretation, some perceived violations are inevitable. One interesting point about the psychological contracting literature is the focus on *employer* violation. Rousseau offers evidence from a longitudinal study of MBA students, over half of which report employer violations of preemployment commitments within the first two years.[38] Perceived violations ranged from inadequate training to discrepancies between promised and actual compensation and promotions to misrepresentations about the nature of the work, degree of job security, or types of co-workers. Since perceived violations are inevitable, a primary task for firms, especially their human resource strategies, is to manage worker expectations and beliefs in order to minimize adverse reactions. Human resource policies seen as clear and fair can help preserve strong relationships (and hence trust and performance) even in the face of perceived violations.[39]

Once again, the notion of workers of integrity is consistent with the psychological contracting literature. Rousseau suggests that people keep their promises (to perform) for any of a number of reasons: goal setting, self-image, to prevent loss to another, social pressure, and incentives. Self-image, in particular, means that people will try to act in a way that maintains consistency between their view of themselves and their acts, which is closely aligned with the coherence requirement of integrity. As in the capabilities literature that focuses on the social nature of the firm, what the notion of worker integrity adds is the commitment to moral principles. The psychological contracting idea especially focuses on the relationship between the employer and employee, and the perils of divergent expectations and beliefs. Workers of integrity have reason to provide their best performances even in ambiguous circumstances and against their other interests. The chances for expected per-

37. A fourth type of contract, *transitional,* characterizes organizations in turmoil where ambiguity, turnover, and instability are all high.

38. Rousseau 1995, 115–17.

39. Like other social commentators, Rousseau (1995, chapter 8) worries that the era of downsizing and high mobility will diminish loyalty to such an extent as to make relational and balanced contracting much more difficult, if not impossible. Also see Sennett 1998.

formance fulfillment increase with contract clarity and fairness, across all contract and firm types.

Finally, Linda Trevino appeals directly to Kohlberg's cognitive moral development theory, an important psychological basis for commitment-integrity discussed in chapter 3, to analyze ethical decision making in firms.[40] She cites evidence that points to a positive relationship between the level of moral reasoning and moral behavior in business situations.[41] She then considers three factors that might contribute to higher moral reasoning in firms. First comes the nature of work itself, borrowing directly from Kohlberg who also considered the issue. Since work constitutes an environment for cognitive interactions, moral reasoning may increase with chances for role-taking opportunities in which others' perspectives are considered, and also chances to take responsibility for resolving moral dilemmas. Second, firm members can be exposed to moral training and education. Much evidence suggests that such exposure increases moral reasoning. Third, evidence also suggests that moral reasoning increases with group decision processes and principled leadership (I will return to these last two points in chapter 9). While I assume that the integrity of workers is given, Trevino suggests ways of increasing it through moral reasoning. That addition is welcome. She also offers a cautionary conclusion in writing: "The evidence thus far suggests that managerial work in business settings may not support moral reasoning at one's cognitive moral development capacity. Powerful organizational norms, reward systems, and structures may serve to constrain or even retard moral reasoning."[42] Once again it would seem that firms may sometimes miss the opportunity to harness the benefits from principled behavior.

6.6. Conclusion

This chapter underscores the proposition that workers of integrity are empirically relevant and consistent with both the capabilities theory of the firm and the psychological contracting literature in organization theory. In contrast, the prominent theories of the firm—transaction cost and agency—are too reliant on the behavioral assumption of opportunism, for which there is scant evidence, and are fundamentally at odds with both the notion of workers of integrity and other motivations for which there is persuasive evidence. The primary implication of the existence of workers of integrity is that firms

40. Trevino 1992.
41. Trevino 1992, 452–53.
42. Trevino 1992, 456.

should create clear and fair agreements. This implication stands in sharp contrast to the transaction cost and agency approaches, with their emphasis on monitoring, incentive contracts, and hierarchy.

So why does opportunism continue to be the sole behavioral workhorse for much of the literature? One reason is methodological simplicity. An economist may reason that if only one behavioral assumption could be made, it might as well be the one most consistent with the practice of utility theory. I have already emphasized my own preference for methodological realism.

Another answer centers on a bias that might apply to both managers as well as economists. One study finds evidence of an "extrinsic incentive bias," a bias where people predict that others are more motivated by extrinsic incentives than they are themselves, and less so by intrinsic motivations.[43] This bias leads managers and principals of organizations to use human resource strategies that focus on the wrong motivation. It might also explain, at least in part, economists' reluctance to consider a richer motivational mix.

Creating clear, fair agreements with their members would benefit all organizations, from the most transactional to the most relational. Clear and fair agreements would give workers of integrity reason to perform and would reduce the chances of rationalized transgressions. Clear and fair agreements also promote trust and loyalty, so that whatever perceived violations do occur are not as destructive as they would be otherwise. As mentioned in literatures from intrinsic motivation to cognitive moral development, one way to ensure such agreements is to use participatory decision processes. Moreover, the emerging evidence suggests that firms that use innovative management practices enjoy greater productivity.[44] Giving workers and members a voice not only confers a measure of control but also provides credible evidence of procedural fairness. Such participation may aid moral reasoning, which is good for both organizations and individuals as well.

So far we have been working mostly with the minimalist moral principle and mutual deceit. We now consider an agreement that necessitates moving beyond these important ideas.

---

43. Heath 1999.

44. Ichniowski and Shaw 2003. Such practices include problem-solving teams, job rotation, screening workers for "team skills," increased training, employment guarantees, information sharing, and incentive pay, both individual and team-based. (Incentive schemes properly designed can augment procedurally fair organizational practices in the sense that those contributing more get higher rewards.) Even traditional hierarchically organized firms using mass assembly-line production are increasingly using these practices, in steel and automobile manufacture, for instance. These practices serve not only to harness existing alternative motivations but also to generate and facilitate the flow of knowledge inside of firms.

Chapter 7

Religious Agreements: Beyond the Minimalist Principle

Religious people seem to do odd things.[1] They sometimes shave their heads, pray a lot, and refrain from eating and consuming things they would otherwise enjoy. Some are gentle and compassionate, while others seem especially prone to intolerance and violence. In this chapter I will describe how the notion of religious integrity could explain otherwise anomalous behavior, and also how adding more principles into the analysis raises new and different problems of incoherence. While most of this book has focused on the parsimonious, minimalist, ethical principle "lying is wrong," a principle virtually all religions profess to be true, the case of religion offers a particularly instructive examination of a wider set of principles because of the important position religion holds in so many people's lives. In this chapter the issue of coherence takes center stage.

The first thing to note is that religious commitment often provides an important source of personal identity.[2] Religions typically provide followers with principles and associated norms, institutions, values, and traditions that enable an individual to establish and maintain a secure identity. Buddhism centers on suffering and its cessation, while Christianity, Hinduism, Islam, and Judaism focus on God and matters like sin and salvation, the nature of reality, service, charity, love, and justice. Each doctrine offers a set of principles whose validity can be judged. Sometimes individuals claim the absolute truth of some principle(s), while at other times they profess *faith* in the veracity of the principle. But if an individual takes religious principles to be true, and if she also judges them to be of sufficient importance that she commits herself to them, then not only could they form an important source of her identity, but she would also have specific reasons for her religious acts. That is, reli-

1. Some of the material in this chapter is adapted from Cosgel and Minkler 2004a and 2004b. However, in those papers we use different levels of commitment to drive the analysis, while in this chapter I focus more on the strength of will.
2. See, for instance, Seul 1999.

gious integrity would give her reason to act in accordance with her religious principles.

One who believes in the truth of religious principles may act counter to her preferences. Almost all religions teach regard for others, something that can be quite difficult to practice, especially in the face of needling preferences that favor pettiness, retribution, or just a general lack of concern. Moreover, religious doctrines usually involve norms and institutional rules that followers are expected to follow. Devout Christians and Jews are expected to observe the Sabbath quite irrespective of any dominant preference to play golf. Devout Muslims are required to pray five times a day, and Islamists believe it impermissible to charge interest on loans. Many religions also impose consumption restrictions. Hindus, Jains, and most Buddhists are expected to eschew meat. Muslims and Jews are not allowed to eat pork. Catholics are not supposed to eat meat on Fridays during Lent. While some may choose to commit simply to the core principles of a religion, many extend their commitments to the associated norms. Their religious integrity encompasses all of it.

To explore these issues I will first review the economic theory of religion. It turns out that an analysis based on religious integrity does not suffer some of the literature's limitations. Then I will offer an extension of chapter 3's analysis by including additional principles and continuous actions. As in chapter 3, the strength of the will is an important determinant of behavior. The chapter concludes with an examination of the different kinds of possible incoherence that a more complicated analysis implies.

7.1. The Economic Theory of Religion

To motivate the discussion on religious behavior, consider the prohibition of the consumption of pork in both Islam and Judaism.[3] Followers of both religions know about the prohibition, and most observe it strictly. Yet others do not. Some will occasionally eat pork, especially if it's the only alternative, while still others will eat it with gusto and regularity. How do economists explain the consumption institution and the behavioral choices of the religions' followers?

While economic perspectives on religion can be traced back to at least Adam Smith, a recent resurgence focuses on three types of explanations.[4] The

3. For the history of the prohibition, see Lobban 1994.

4. See Anderson 1988; Welch and Mueller 2001; Iannaccone 1998; also the 1992 special issue (vol. 150, no. 4) of the *Journal of Institutional and Theoretical Economics.*

first focuses on a religion's influence on preference formation. Raised as Jews or Muslims, followers' preferences evolve until they no longer favor pork; pork becomes inferior to the available alternatives. Economists are usually skeptical of this kind of preference account to explain choice. To say that people don't eat pork because they don't like it is not really saying much.[5] And, historically, economists have not wanted to venture into the realm of preference formation, believing it instead to be an area best investigated by other social sciences. Still, careful study of endogenous preference formation may be able explain a lot of important behavior, like cooperation. Many scholars who favor evolutionary methodology are pursuing that research agenda.[6] But I am unaware of any work that convincingly draws a link between the choice of religion and its effects on preference formation for things like participation in religious rituals and the consumption of pork.

The second economic approach to explain religious behavior focuses on incentives and opportunity sets. Perhaps the most interesting idea that uses this basic approach and applies it to religion comes from Laurence Iannaccone.[7] He models religious organizations as quasi-public clubs. In his analysis, benefits to each religious member derive from the fellowship of others; each member's consumption of a religious good depends on the intensity and earnestness of other members' contributions like greetings, singing, praying, and so on. Thus religious members both produce and consume fellowship. The economic problem centers on how to prevent free riders from joining, that is, those who would enjoy the benefits of consuming fellowship without paying its costs. How could a religious organization prevent membership by one who wants to receive warm greetings but not give them? The answer borrows from the signaling literature. That is, religions can require seemingly irrelevant behaviors in order to signal the willingness of members to contribute to fellowship. Those most willing to contribute would also be most likely to engage in other behaviors that might be seen as costly.[8] Thus a Jew refrains from eating pork in order to signal her willingness to contribute to the quality of her synagogue, and other members reaffirm that membership based on their observations of that signal.[9]

5. Frank's (1997a, 215) treatment of crankcase oil was discussed in chapter 2, this volume. Why did the man drink crankcase oil and then keel over and die? He must have really *liked* crankcase oil.

6. See, for instance, Bowles 1998.

7. See Iannaccone 1998.

8. For Iannaccone, those most likely to absorb the cost of these signals would also likely be those that have fewer secular market alternatives. But that position doesn't seem necessary.

9. Anthropologists offer perhaps a more sophisticated signaling account. On that view, religious behavior promotes cooperative behavior, which yields evolutionary advantages. Costly rituals are signals that facilitate beneficial group formation. See, for instance, Sosis and Alcorta 2003.

The third and final class of economic explanation focuses on social norms and constraints. The idea here is that after joining some social group, one then submits to its informal and formal rules. If one becomes a Muslim, for instance, one agrees to abide by the norm not to eat pork. That norm is enforced by social pressure in social situations. The reactions from an observant Muslim to a pork-eating one could range from a disapproving glance to stern verbal admonishment. The unpleasantness of any public disapproval could thus serve as a sufficient deterrent, or constraint, to prevent an otherwise pork-loving Muslim from consuming it in public.[10] The further prospect of other Muslims finding out about the transgression provides even further deterrence. The origination of the norm in the first place is not central to such analyses.

All of these approaches have merit and undoubtedly explain some religious behavior. However, each also has its own limitations. For instance, while some version of the (endogenous) preference account could probably explain why individuals would come to attach positive utility from worship and other rituals like singing and dancing, it is not apparent how it could explain other rituals like fasting or observing Lenten prohibitions, which, by their very nature, are supposed to be utility reducing. It is also not clear how someone who has never tasted pork in her life could form complete preferences over it. As far as the other approaches go, neither the signaling nor the social norm accounts can explain why religious individuals would still take counterpreferred actions in private. If a Jew likes pork, but only refrains from eating it in public so as to avoid social sanction from a valued peer group or to signal to others her willingness to make religious contributions, she should also happily devour swine when she is dining alone. Yet many, perhaps most, Jews and Muslims do not alter their religious behavior even when they are alone. Less committed ones may alter their behavior sometimes, but the most devout ones surely do not.

7.2. Religious Integrity

For an alternative account of religious behavior, consider religious integrity and its requirements. First, an individual must take a religious doctrine to be

10. For example, Kuran's (1990, 1995) work on preference falsification gives various examples of how social pressure might cause an individual to choose differently in public than in private. Historically, preference falsification has sometimes been necessary in order to preserve one's faith. During the time of the Spanish Inquisition, many Jews feigned conversion to Christianity in public, while continuing to practice their Jewish faith in the privacy of their own homes (Kuran 1995, 6–7). Interestingly, Judaic law permitted such lies in the face of danger, in order to prevent or reduce the greater harm of annihilating the religion.

true. Religious doctrines specify principles and associated prescribed actions. Next, the individual must commit to that doctrine and identify with it. In that way religious integrity gives the agent reason to act according to the accepted religious principles. In this simple account, which will shortly be complicated with the notion of multidimensional identity, failures to act with integrity could only stem from a weakness of will.

Before developing this idea further, since this book is about integrity *and* agreements, it is necessary to consider who the parties are to a religious agreement. When considering the minimalist principle of "lying is wrong," the agreement was always between the promisor and a distinct promisee (e.g., contractual partner, constituent, boss). In the present case, followers are often asked to agree to the religion's formal and informal rules. The promisee could be other followers, religious authorities, God, or any combination.[11] To break such an agreement one never intended to honor would be to lie, and to violate the minimalist moral principle found in virtually all religions.

Of course there are different levels of commitment, so there are different levels of agreement. Upholding moral principles can be difficult no matter what one's level of commitment, however, which is why most religions have some provision for forgiveness. This is not to say that religious followers will not keep their agreements; if a follower is to act with religious integrity then there is immediate reason to do so. But it's also at least possible that a follower doesn't make any agreements, yet she still acts with religious integrity. In such a case it is simply the perceived truth of the religious principles themselves that give the reason to act. This possibility exists especially for nontheistic religions. For instance, Taoists need only accord with The Way, the natural source of all things, without any further reference to a social community or a higher being.[12] The big issue to consider in the move beyond the minimalist moral principle to religious ones is that there are now a number of prescribed and proscribed acts, each of which could be engaged at different levels. The issue is no longer just to lie or not to lie, but whether to eat pork and, if so, how much; whether to engage in premarital sex and, if so, how much; whether to pray and, if so, how much; and so on.

We can formalize a bit the idea of religious integrity by extending the analysis of chapter 3. As before, let $\mathbf{x}$ denote the action vector taken by the in-

11. God may not be harmed by a lie, but the liar committed to God is.

12. See Lao-tzu's *Tao Te Ching* (1988). Religions like Taoism and Buddhism are interesting because they maintain that the ultimate truth can only be attained by giving up notions of a personal identity or separate self. Thus a realized Taoist or Buddhist could not identify with religious principles because identity is vacuous. Such individuals are beyond integrity. Still, lesser practitioners do retain a personal identity on the way to enlightenment, and thus are candidates for religious integrity.

dividual. The individual has well-behaved preferences that obey the usual assumptions, so she has a unique utility-maximizing choice denoted by $\mathbf{x}^*$. Religious considerations are formulated as follows. The religious doctrine prescribes or proscribes either unique actions, denoted by $\mathbf{x}^r$ (refrain from pork eating, refrain from premarital sex, pray five times a day, give tithe of $1,000 per month, etc.), or no specific actions, in which case the individual is free to maximize utility. For instance, $x_1^r = x_2^r = 0$, but $x_3^r = 5$ and $x_4^r = 1{,}000$; so there could be many prescribed actions of continuous amounts. For now, suppose that $\mathbf{x}^* \neq \mathbf{x}^r$, so that the individual does not prefer the required actions. The actual choice of the follower with religious integrity, $\mathbf{x}'$, depends on her strength of will, denoted by μ.[13] The strength of will is indexed so it can be compared to the difference between the utility of those actions that maximize utility and those required by religious principles taken to be true, or $U(\mathbf{x}^*) - U(\mathbf{x}^r)$.

Given these considerations, there are now three possibilities for any given act. Suppose that $x_i^r = x$, where x is some nonnegative number. First, if $\mu > U(x_i) - U(x_i^r = x)$ for all $x_i \neq x$, then $x_i' = x$. In this case, the person of religious integrity has the strength of will to choose the action prescribed by her religion, the tenets of which she has accepted as truth. She prays five times a day and refrains from eating pork in both public and private. Second, if $\mu < U(x_i) - U(x)$ for all $x_i \neq x$, then $x_i' = x^*$. Now the religious follower cannot will the act prescribed; instead she chooses her preferred action, which is to eat pork with abandon. Finally, to include intermediate activity levels, for some activity level x^z, if $\mu > U(x^z + \varepsilon) - U(x)$ *and* $\mu < U(x^z - \varepsilon) - U(x)$, for some sufficiently small ε, then $x' = x^z$.[14] In this case, the religious follower has intermediate strength of will and chooses an act that represents a compromise between her religion's dictates and her own preferences.

When we consider all possible acts, we see that a given strength of will may be sufficient to assure some prescribed acts, but not others. Some devout religious followers may have the strength of will to follow *all* prescribed and proscribed acts. But others, with weaker wills, may engage in less consistent behavior. For instance, some follower may be able to refrain from premarital sex altogether but can only muster praying three times a day, and has such a weakness for pork that she eats as much as she wants, at least in private.[15] For

13. To keep the focus on multiple principles and continuous actions, assume away other problems such as errors in judgment, self-deception, and moral exclusion. The last issue in particular deserves further treatment; I will touch on it again at the end of this chapter.

14. Assuming that U is concave in $\mathbf{x}$, then x^z is a unique solution if $x = 0$, a local solution otherwise.

15. Note that I am assuming that the strength of will is given and the same for each act; it never grows weaker or stronger as new acts are taken. A fuller analysis might include the possibility of a weakening will as one takes tempting actions and a strengthening one as one practices restraint.

this individual, there is incoherence between some of her actions and a doctrine she takes to be true, so she could not be said to be a religious follower of integrity.

While the analysis here provides an entirely separable reason for religious choices, other approaches can easily be accommodated into this framework. For instance, those that explain choices as resulting from preferences, either exogenous or endogenous, can be accommodated by relaxing the assumption that $\mathbf{x}^* \neq \mathbf{x}^r$. If instead an individual preferred what her religion required, so that $\mathbf{x}^* = \mathbf{x}^r$, then $\mathbf{x}' = \mathbf{x}^* = \mathbf{x}^r$ for all μ. Now any will, even no will at all, could lead to $\mathbf{x}^r$. Even though the resulting action is the same as an account that relies only on preferences, the one here is more nuanced because it also includes religious integrity, required actions, and the strength of will. If the follower is a person of integrity, it is her chosen principles that account for her actions, not her preferences. It is also a simple matter to include social pressure. If an individual experiences social pressure from choosing a *public* action different from $\mathbf{x}^r$, then the utility associated with $\mathbf{x}^*$ decreases.[16] That means for any given strength of will μ, the chosen action $\mathbf{x}'$ will more closely approximate $\mathbf{x}^r$ because it more closely approximates the preferred action. The more disutility from social pressure the individual experiences, the weaker the will has to be to practice required religious actions. Social pressure could help followers with weaker wills to act with integrity. Similarly, social pressure against religious doctrine would require a stronger will because now the utility associated with $\mathbf{x}^*$ increases.

This simple framework can be used to describe all kinds of religious consumption choices, for example, the decision between devoting time to worship and leisure, acts of charity and violence, and so on. However, something more is needed to describe certain religious consumption, namely, that which seems specifically geared toward an audience.[17] There are many examples of such religious expression. For example, Muslim women wear headscarves, and Jewish men wear yarmulkes. Other religious expressions include distinctive styles of clothing, grooming, and jewelry (e.g., necklaces with a cross). Sometimes small differences in the style, size, or shape of religious consumption can make significant statements. For instance, a Muslim woman can express her religious commitment by how well her headscarf covers her hair, as well as by its style and color.

To explain the kind of religious consumption aimed at an audience, we

16. Remember that the social pressure approach cannot explain counterpreferred private choices that accord with religious requirements.

17. This is the topic of Cosgel and Minkler 2004b.

need to add one further assumption. We assume that some who have committed to religious principles *also* need to express that commitment. This need is analogous to expressive utility, or the desire to publicize one's private *preferences.*[18] Obviously not all followers need to express their commitment; many prefer to keep their worship or spirituality private. But for those who need to express their commitment, including its intensity, religious consumption norms facilitate that kind of expression. Consumption norms provide the language, rules, and constraints to communicate meaning. That's why a Muslim woman can express her belief by wearing a headscarf and express the intensity of her belief by how she wears the headscarf and what type she wears. She is not at liberty to use a flowered hat or necklace for the same purpose. Moreover, the audience is not at liberty to interpret her headscarf as a sign of her marital status, political affiliation, or ethnic identity. Religious consumption norms make the meaning of the expression precise.

7.3. Multidimensional Identity and Incoherence

We have been considering the requirements for a religious person of integrity. Previously, we considered a person of integrity based on the minimalist moral principle of "lying is wrong." Of course, a person could be both. But why stop there? Since we have allowed the inclusion of religious principles, why not other kinds? And why confine commitments to just principles? As Bernard Williams says, "one can be committed to such things as a person, a cause, an institution, a career, one's own genius, or the pursuit of danger."[19] It is easy to envision a person who is committed to being honest, religious, a good parent, spouse, worker, friend, community member, and so on. Each one of these things could jointly constitute a person's identity and sense of self. The point of focusing on the minimalist principle was to keep the theory parsimonious, but now that we have moved beyond the simple framework we can at least point to the problem of incoherence associated with multiple commitments.

Until now, we mostly focused on the incoherence between accepted principle and act. With the inclusion of additional commitments, three new kinds of incoherence can emerge. First, chosen principles can sometimes conflict. I previously touched on this case in discussing the choice one could have if a prospective murderer asked the whereabouts of a child. In that case the principle of "not lying" could conflict with "not causing harm." As another exam-

18. Kuran 1995, 31

19. Smart and Williams 1973, 112.

ple, an artist may confront a conflict between "art for art's sake" and a religious principle forbidding works it considers to be obscene or idolatrous. In these multiple principle cases, an act in accordance with one principle might violate another. One way out of this apparent dilemma, at least when there appears to be a conflict between moral principles, is to consider the conflict to be between prima facie principles, where the true principle reveals itself at the time of action.[20] For most of us, "not causing harm" would most likely reveal itself as the true principle if we found ourselves in the difficult circumstance mentioned earlier.

A second, related, source of incoherence can arise if principles and another commitment conflict. Commitments are often complementary, particularly when the minimalist principle is involved. One who is honest and brings that disposition to parenting, work, and relationships with others will go some way to meeting the requirements of those identities. However, a potential problem arises if the commitments associated with one identity conflict with the commitments of another, or if the required acts conflict. For instance, being a good employee may mean doing what's good for one's employer, while being a good friend means treating their interests as your own. If the friend is a co-worker whose interests are harmed by the company's interests (e.g., layoffs), holding commitments to both the friend and company may be quite impossible. A person of integrity thus could not hold both commitments simultaneously without suffering a form of incoherence.

The third source of incoherence, perhaps the most problematic, centers on multiple required acts. This problem has been called "moral overload."[21] The source of the problem is that time constraints limit the ability to perform some acts at the expense of others. So even if the acts required from identifying as a devoted artist don't conflict with those of being a devoted mother, wife, community member, and religious follower, time limitations may prevent performing certain acts required by certain commitments. An artist who holds "art for art's sake" may not have the time to also be a good mother and friend. Incoherence results because the required acts associated with being a good mother and friend cannot be performed, even if the individual meets the other requirements for integrity and has the sufficient will to act; there is simply not enough time (and perhaps resources).

While the minimalist moral principle just requires refraining from lying, something that generally doesn't require too much time, the inclusion of added principles and commitments will often require additional actions.

20. This is the solution offered by Ross (1939).
21. Kuran 1998.

Some won't; refraining from eating pork will generally not require additional time. But praying five times a day, giving tithe, creating art, being a good parent, being a good employee, and so on all require positive, time-consuming actions. In the extreme case of someone like Don Quixote, holding so many commitments to promote the highest good, while admirable, may even prove a bit dysfunctional—the Don Quixote syndrome! In any case, time constraints would seem to limit the number of commitments a person of integrity could coherently hold.

Concluding Comment

We have seen how moving beyond the minimalist principle can help to explain some behaviors that are difficult for the usual explanations, for instance certain counterpreferential religious behavior in private. That certainly does not mean that other explanations are not useful for many kinds of behavior. Many people probably join religious groups precisely for the contacts or country club memberships made possible. Of course such people cannot be said to be persons of integrity. Moreover, for those individuals who are of integrity but who also hold additional commitments, we have seen that they confront a greater possibility of incoherence.

I also want to at least recognize one problem I have glossed over. To keep the analysis of religious integrity focused, I assumed away the problem of moral exclusion. That issue is important, however, because sometimes religion and religious identity help to foster insider-outsider distinctions. Sometimes followers, by bastardizing a religion's tenets, rationalize moral exclusion of *outsiders* in order to commit immoral acts. Wars and crimes of the highest order have been rationalized in this way throughout human history. But as Sissela Bok argues in her treatise on lying, moral exclusion is very rarely justified, and only then if it can prevent great harm.

The next chapter on the social contract and human rights takes up the issue of preventing great harm, with coherence again playing a central role.

Chapter 8

The Social Contract and Human Rights

By two roads man comes nearest to God: by always speaking the truth, and by doing good to others.[1]

This chapter considers the normative relationship between integrity and the social contract, specifically a human rights–based social contract. A social contract is an agreement between individuals that metes out rights and obligations, and justifies various roles for political entities. Individuals may largely be anonymous to one another, but interrelated nevertheless because of the need for interaction. The social contract provides the foundations for social relationships between individuals who would otherwise live a solitary (or relatively solitary) existence in the "state of nature." For self-interested individuals, a fundamental question concerns whether to consent and conform to such a contract because of the constraints it imposes on liberties and obligations. The more relevant question for this study asks what constraints, if any, are imposed on a person of integrity in terms of her support of and adherence to the social contract. It turns out that coherence, one of the primary themes of this book, requires a person of integrity to support human rights so long as the principle(s) upon which integrity are based, even a minimalist one like "lying is wrong," contain a causal link to the importance of human dignity.[2] Human rights are explicitly founded on human dignity. We begin by looking briefly at human rights and then proceed to the argument linking integrity and human rights.

8.1. Human Rights

At the most fundamental level, social contract theory provides the moral bases and implied duties for governments. In his classic work *Leviathan*, Thomas

1. Saying attributed to Pythagoras, quoted in Hugo Grotius's *The Law of War and Peace* (1949, bk. 3, chapter 1, 281).
2. So, for instance, instead of basing a principle on a proposition like "lying is wrong," it is necessary that it be based on a proposition like "lying is wrong *because it violates human dignity.*" The added clause is what coherence works on to assure that the individual also must support and adhere to human rights.

Hobbes values peace and stability above all else and describes how starting from the state of nature, members of society can achieve those things by voluntarily submitting to a sovereign. John Locke, Jean-Jacques Rousseau, and John Rawls all start with human liberty and equality, and through some kind of philosophical device arrive at particular rights of individuals and duties of governments.[3] While consent by members in each type of social contract is hypothetical, rational individuals would consent to them in order to create the implied institutions and, in so doing, realize the rights and duties therein. A just government enjoys an intellectual basis in social contract theory; an unjust one does not. Thus social contract theory provides the justification for a certain kind of government, if not the real-life version in question.

Human rights, first as an intellectual idea and then as embodied in the Universal Declaration of Human Rights and its subsequent covenants, constitutes a social contract. The Universal Declaration of Human Rights was adopted by the UN General Assembly in 1948. It, too, is founded on a moral basis, involves consent, and assigns rights and duties. Human dignity provides the primary moral foundation for human rights. In principle, human rights are the product of what moral individuals would consent to. In practice, as signatories to international treaties, nation-states have actually consented to be held accountable to the international community. Human rights also establish the requirements for a just government. As usually conceived of, individual citizens as rights holders are entitled to certain obligations from their governments, both negative (e.g., not to infringe upon enumerated liberties) and positive (e.g., to provide social security and adequate standard of living). However, if human rights are to be truly universal, then individuals themselves may possess duties to those both within and beyond their own borders as well.[4] Thus human rights might be seen to demand difficult responsibilities.[5]

The field of human rights is marked by debates over whether rights conflict, are unattainable because of resource constraints, or otherwise im-

3. For a good summary, see the listing for "social contract" in *Oxford Companion to Philosophy,* edited by Ted Honderich. The other classic works are Locke's *Two Treatises of Government,* Rousseau's *Social Contract,* and Rawls's (1971) *A Theory of Justice.*

4. While it is usually argued that human rights only impose obligations on governments, others like Copp (1992) argue that individuals have the responsibility to support required government actions by paying taxes. Still others, like Thomas Pogge (2002), argue that advantaged citizens in affluent countries are actively responsible for the crushing poverty experienced by hundreds of millions around the world. His argument is that because we create and benefit from an international economic system that violates the basic duty not to harm others (a negative duty), and there are feasible alternative international arrangements, we are individually responsible.

5. While it is sometimes claimed that human rights are a Western construct, it is perhaps better to view them as a Western articulation of universal ideas. Lauren (1998) convincingly argues that because all major religions and philosophies through time have addressed both the moral worth and

pose onerous obligations, rights inflation, and possible interference with security interests. Some debates concern whether rights are even intellectually justified in the first place. For our purposes, the most fundamental issue concerns the foundation of human rights and its relationship to integrity. The link is dignity. As mentioned, human dignity is often considered to provide foundation for human rights, so we now examine that idea.

Dignity is explicitly identified as the foundation for human rights in the Universal Declaration of Human Rights.[6] Its preamble begins, "Whereas recognition of the inherent dignity and of the equal and inalienable rights of all members of the human family is the foundation of freedom, justice and peace in the world," while the first article starts, "All human beings are born free and equal in dignity and rights." How then is dignity used to justify human rights?

Many start with the ethics of Immanuel Kant. For Kant, the categorical imperative provides the source of the moral law. The second version specifies the duty for rational beings to treat other rational beings as ends, never solely as a means to one's own purposes. That rational agents are ends in themselves means that they possess inherent dignity or intrinsic worth that is not subject to any price, and as such are deserving of equal respect from other rational agents. From this link of dignity and duty of respect comes the correlative right to respect due to rational agents. Human rights are just the embodiment of this right to respect.[7]

A more recent approach reverses the logic and finds rights as the source of dignity, and argues that human need transforms those rights into human rights.[8] From this perspective a right is a sort of claim that exists prior to any

---

responsibility of persons, no one society, culture, or worldview can claim the notion of human rights uniquely as its own. Instead, by each contributing its own vision the possibility was sustained until the current version was articulated. Clearly most societies through time would not adhere to the current conception, but the best thinking of many laid the foundation. The Universal Declaration of Human Rights was the product of the deliberations of delegates that represented a remarkable number of cultures and viewpoints. While important disagreements still exist (which I will allude to presently), many of those too are mere appearance. For instance, Amartya Sen (2001, chapter 10) effectively counters those who would argue that "Asian values" favor discipline and loyalty; thus certain brands of authoritarianism are biased in their selections from Asian doctrines. As a counterexample, Sen offers Buddhism as a doctrine that champions human freedom.

6. Some argue that rights are conferred by law or political struggle, but in actuality they have a more primitive ethical foundation (see Sen 2001, chapter 10).

7. This last link comes from the formulation offered by Gewirth (1996), a fuller description of which follows.

8. This is the approach of Feinberg (1970). Others also invoke need as the basis for human rights. For instance, Copp (1992) argues that each person requires that her basic needs are met in order to secure and provide for her autonomy and rational agency, and the state's obligation to provide for these needs derives from this requirement. Sen (2001) similarly invokes need fulfillment in his

imposed duty. Those who are potential claims-makers can be thought of as possessing dignity, which leaves open the possibility that it is contingent rather than inherent unless all persons could be thought of as potential claims-makers. The reasoning continues that only valid claims constitute rights, with prima facie claims being worthy of consideration. Human need may qualify as one source of validity, making the claim truly a human right.

Alan Gewirth provides a link between dignity and human rights, premised on Kantian ethics.[9] Briefly, he argues that human action presupposes worthy ends or purposes. Those purposes are the result of conscious reflection and are thus volitional. That an agent has worthy ends implies that the agent herself is intrinsically worthy, that is, possesses inherent dignity. Such dignity is not contingent on circumstances because it accrues to agents that act, that is, all agents. Since agents must logically attribute dignity to themselves by virtue of their purposeful action, so too must they attribute that same dignity to all others because of the same general purposeful action of all others. The inherent dignity of all further implies that each is entitled to the rights, human rights, that safeguard the freedom and well-being of agents so that they may act purposefully in the first place. Importantly, human rights constrain the purposes of all, which addresses the potential criticism that agents with bad purposes do not deserve to use actions based on those purposes for the source of their human dignity. Once an agent accepts self-worth based on this reasoning, she must also subscribe to the attendant moral restrictions. An agent who accepts that her purposeful action confers a dignity that must be protected with human rights is not free to violate the same rights of others. To do so would be a form of incoherence.

Before continuing, it might be useful to comment on the scope of what human dignity requires. To say that human dignity underlies human rights does not mean that any harm to dignity or any human requirement must be protected with human rights. Except perhaps in cases where rights conflict, intentional government actions that harm human dignity are indeed human rights violations (e.g., a police officer intentionally harming an innocent is a human rights violation). But individuals do not have the human right to petition their government to prevent their neighbors from being rude. Nor, just because realizing our full humanity requires love and community, does that mean we have a human right to those things. The exact line of demarcation between human dignity and the human rights implied is still debatable, but

---

treatment of welfare and argues for human rights as means to do so (as well as an end unto themselves). If social primary goods are thought of as meeting basic human needs Rawls's (1971) theory of justice can also be seen as a needs-based justification for human rights.

9. See Gewirth 1978, 1992.

human rights inflation needn't follow. Moreover, my aim centers on the more general normative requirements for those whom human dignity provides a motivation to act.

8.2. Coherence, Dignity, and Human Rights

Most of the discussion in this book has relied on the minimalist principle of "lying is wrong" for the conception of integrity, with implications coming more from the concepts of mutual deceit and coherence. By itself, it is not clear yet how that minimalist principle could provide a link between integrity and the social contract of human rights. On the surface it would seem that one could accept the principle as true but have no particular view either of human rights or of a social contract more generally.

To establish a link, it is necessary to ask why an individual would take the minimalist principle to be true. There could be myriad reasons, but we can focus on just a few different classes, namely, those based on self-interest, God's will, and harm to others. First, consider self-interest. In that case one may accept as true that "lying is wrong because if caught I might get punished or forgo future benefits." While many individuals may not lie because of that motivation, the person of integrity, at least the person of commitment-integrity, is not at liberty to act on such an instrumentally rational principle. Such a person of integrity cannot adopt a principle that provides motivation that cannot go against self-interest. In the present case the added clause makes the "wrongness" of lying contingent on one's own interests. Something is wrong if it goes against one's interests, right if it supports one's own interests. That notion of wrongness is thus equivalent to instrumental rationality and not permissible for the person of integrity.[10]

All major religions prohibit lying, at least in normal circumstances. That prohibition, in turn, could be based on God's will or preventing harm (discussed later). But for some individuals the first class of reasons might expand the minimalist principle to "lying is wrong because it is against God's will." The presumption is that God's will is "good." But in order to know if a link exists between the truth of this principle and human rights, one would need to know more about God's will, in particular what God's will requires. If God's will is good, and if it further requires adherence to human rights, then a per-

10. Similarly, an individual might believe the principle "lying is wrong" to be true but act on the self-interested motivation, that is, to avoid punishment or to reap benefits. That describes an external (as opposed to internal) reason for acting and thus once again is not permissible for the person of integrity (see chapter 3, this volume).

son of integrity could not coherently accept the truth of the expanded principle and also oppose human rights. While it seems reasonable to assume that God's will would include not harming others, there may be other interpretations, so I leave that case and proceed to the third, which links integrity to human rights directly.

In her seminal treatise, Sissela Bok suggests that lying is akin to violence because both cause harm and can coerce victims to act against their will. Stated a little differently, lying can reduce the freedom and well-being of the person who has been lied to. Anyone who is lied to suffers a type of harm. The question then becomes, why is harming wrong for the person of integrity? Is harming another always wrong? In the case of torture, for example, some would argue that harming another to prevent even greater harm is not only morally permissible but morally required. I will discuss that case presently, but if "harming is wrong" is to be a general principle it cannot be contingent. Even in the case of torture, the purported rightness of the act stems from its ability to prevent (even greater) harm. Harm is still presumed to be wrong.

One candidate for why harming is wrong, perhaps the only reasonable one, is that it violates another's intrinsic worth—her dignity. If people possess intrinsic worth they are entitled to not have their freedom and well-being violated, at least insofar as their freedom and well-being do not infringe on others. It is quite natural therefore to consider lying wrong because of the harm it causes to another's dignity. So, in this third case, the minimalist principle expands to "lying is wrong because it causes harm, and harming is wrong because it violates human dignity." I will mostly use the shorter version: "lying is wrong because it violates human dignity." Based on internal reasons (discussed in chapter 3), the truth of that principle supplies the motivation for not lying. Coherence then requires the person of integrity who embraces that version of the "not lying" principle to also embrace human rights (at least generally conceived) because both rest on human dignity.

This principle presumes that dignity is a good end. The connection is direct because all that it implies is that intrinsic human worth is worthy. Thus the full principle should read: "lying is wrong because it causes harm, and harming is wrong because it violates human dignity, and human dignity is good." The formulation also employs an inherent rather than contingent notion of dignity. While some may attribute dignity only to those who are honest, brave, or hold an esteemed position, that kind of view could not consistently provide the foundation for the preceding principle. Using the contingent form of dignity would transform that principle into "lying is wrong because it causes harm (in all), and harming is wrong because it violates the human dignity (of some)." Perhaps this principle could be modified to justify not lying to some, while some other version of the principle (not founded on dignity) could justify not lying to others. But so long as one believes that harming all is wrong, contingent dignity cannot provide the basis for "lying is wrong."

In order to assess the link between integrity and human rights, we need to first differentiate between different kinds of human rights. Typically, that is done by distinguishing "negative" from "positive" rights.[11] Negative human rights imply negative obligations. So, for instance, one person's negative human right to be free from torture necessitates the correlative obligation for government (and perhaps other individuals) not to torture. Negative obligations thus prohibit certain acts. In contrast, positive human rights imply positive obligations. The negative/positive distinction has been convincingly challenged by human rights scholars, most fundamentally because the fulfillment of all human rights requires both actions and resources.[12] Still, I will maintain the distinction for the purposes of the following discussion. Since positive human rights are more controversial, and the link between integrity and negative human rights is more obvious, I start there first.

Suppose a person of integrity accepts the truth of the principle "lying is wrong because it violates human dignity." Could that person also support the proposition (and the act stemming from it) "torture is acceptable to extract information"? Generally speaking no, because torture violates human dignity, and coherence requires the person of integrity embracing the minimalist principle to not violate human dignity. Our emotional disposition toward the person holding the information is not particularly relevant, because she too must be viewed as possessing inherent (rather than contingent) dignity. As mentioned, some might argue that other more compelling reasons, preventing great harm, for instance, might override maintaining moral integrity.

In unusual circumstances a person of integrity may have to grapple with such a conflict, particularly if she also holds more extensive moral principles like "stop great suffering whenever I can." Kant held that there could be no exceptions to the "not lying" principle and, by extension, "not torturing," because to do otherwise would cause harm to another's dignity for which the violator would be morally responsible. The moral responsibility for the great harm not prevented by not torturing the informant would rest solely with the

11. For one of the myriad sources, see Gewirth 1996, chapter 2.

12. See Shue 1980; Sunstein 2004. For example, the right to noninterference requires the government to actively invest in police, courts, prisons, and so on. Shue introduced the idea that all human rights include the duties to *avoid* depriving people of their needs, to *protect* them from deprivation, and to *aid* them when so deprived. For discussion of many of the issues surrounding economic and social rights ("positive rights"), see Beetham 1995; Hertel and Minkler 2007.

perpetrators, because they are the ones who caused the harm. As I have mentioned in earlier chapters, other philosophers are not so ironclad. For instance, W. D. Ross argued that what appear to be conflicting obligations are really just conflicting prima facie obligations, and that at the time of decision one would intuitively reveal itself to be the true obligation or duty.[13] It is worth noting that all of the important human rights documents make no exceptions. Torture is forbidden in all circumstances—inherent human dignity reigns supreme.

So, absent the other kinds of considerations just mentioned, a person of integrity has a duty not to torture, or not to support an agent torturing on her behalf, because to do otherwise would directly cause harm to another's inherent dignity. The duty for the person of integrity is negative in the sense that she is required not to act or interfere in some harmful way. Most civil and political human rights take this form, that is, they impose negative correlative duties. Thus the person of integrity is not at liberty to engage in discrimination, attack another's honor or reputation, steal their property, deprive them of their right to freedom of thought, conscience, or religion, or support a government that does so.

The link between integrity and negative human rights rests on the negative aspect of the "not lying" principle, its link to human dignity, and coherence. Refraining from lying implies refraining from other kinds of behavior that violate another's dignity. In contrast, the link between integrity and positive human rights rests more on the principle "dignity is good," coherence, and the rights of the claims holder. Because the person of integrity takes "dignity is good" to be true, in general, coherence requires that she is obligated to act (or support government action) in order to fulfill a positive human rights holder's claim. The only other requirement necessary to establish the link is that universal human dignity provides the foundation for human rights in the first place, and that the person of integrity recognizes that foundation. For many, that requirement is likely to be fulfilled for reasons given earlier, namely, that the major human rights documents explicitly mention human dignity as a first principle, but also that both common intuition and intricate philosophical reasoning all point to the link. If the person of integrity recog-

13. Ross 1939. In contrast, Gewirth 1996 offers a "criterion of degrees of needfulness for action" based on the importance of the object of freedom to determine which right gets priority. It's a sort of moral cost-benefit analysis. Of course, Utilitarians would have less trouble with the conflict, tending toward torture if doing so could result in a reasonable chance of preventing great harm. While the moral burden for Utilitarians can be far greater than that for persons of integrity, especially with respect to positive obligations, in general, integrity and Utilitarianism are not compatible (unless a person of integrity happens to embrace Utilitarian principles). See Williams in Smart and Williams 1973.

nizes such a basis, and if a claims holder asserts a positive human right, then the correlative positive obligation must also be recognized. Otherwise, the person of integrity would hold the view that "dignity is good, dignity founds human rights (negative and positive), human rights impose legitimate obligations, yet I am not obligated to act based on those rights and obligations." This statement is incoherent unless the person of integrity can find compelling reason to think that the obligations required by human rights don't apply to her, or don't apply to her in certain circumstances.

Libertarians provide such an exception. Libertarians believe in free will and human worth; humans should be free to act on their wills without interference in order to achieve their own purposes, subject only that they do not interfere with the purposes of others. In general, therefore, libertarians could accept the preceding analysis for negative human rights (civil and political), but not positive ones (economic, social, and cultural). The primary reason is that liberty—the individual's right to noninterference—takes priority, and positive human rights can conflict with that privileged negative right. For example, state taxation policies that promote the economic welfare of some infringe on the property rights of others. So libertarians would hold that no positive duty exists because no positive human right exists, since such a purported right would conflict with another's right of noninterference.

Libertarianism has been harshly criticized.[14] The main attack goes something like this: if actualization of human worth and autonomy are the highest ends, how is it that liberty gets privileged to such an extent that it means that others are unable to achieve even their minimal purposes for want of the most basic necessities? What good is freedom, when one is not free from starvation? To these critics, while the problem of conflicting rights is real, that cannot be the basis for dismissing positive rights when those rights are necessary to achieve the very aims libertarians claim to hold. I am not aware of a compelling response. Still, as a positive matter many people do hold libertarian principles. The preceding normative analysis indicates that those who do must also accept the negative obligations associated with political and civil human rights in order to also be persons of integrity.

For those unable to resolve this criticism and thus accept the existence of positive rights and obligations as true, the question is a practical one: what is one's moral *responsibility* to fulfill positive obligations? Actually, the question is also relevant for negative obligations. While it is fairly clear that one has a moral responsibility not to torture, the question still remains as to how much should one materially provide to their government to stop torture at home

14. For example, see Copp 1992; Gewirth 1996; Sen 2001. Also see Hausman and McPherson 2006.

and abroad. The question may be even more problematic when it comes to how much should one give to poverty relief. We can identify three factors that would lessen, or could be perceived to lessen, one's responsibility: personal circumstances, incentives, and degree of cause. The first factor concerns one's ability to fulfill an obligation; the poor cannot reasonably be expected to contribute a large share of their own resources in order to fulfill obligations to others. Even if one is well-off, it is not clear how much to give and to whom. Since human rights are universal, is the Portuguese patron responsible to meet the legitimate claims of a Canadian Inuit? Both philosophically and practically, these are difficult questions.

Social welfare programs can diminish productivity. Economists are quick to point out that if a person can be sure that their material needs will be met whatever their own productive efforts, that person has less incentive to provide those efforts in the first place. While the degree to which incentives are necessary to assure effort is debatable, and the benefits of social insurance sometimes underappreciated, certainly the person of integrity is not required to support social insurance to the degree that it overwhelmingly retards productive efforts.[15]

The degree of cause is the third determinant of responsibility. In the case of a positive obligation like providing an adequate standard of living, the person of integrity can at best be thought of as an indirect cause of an impoverished person's plight. Other causes could include bad luck, social factors like racism, and/or poor choices by the impoverished person herself. A person of integrity may be able to condition the degree of her support on the perceived causes of the impoverished person's plight.

In many instances, it could be argued that an individual's obligation is only indirect; the direct obligation applies to the state, and the individual's role is to provide resources somehow proportional to ability so that the state can meet its positive obligation.[16] Perhaps the most compelling solution would arise from an informed public debate, which could take into consideration all of the relevant factors of time and place.[17] Such a solution would start from the existence of a positive obligation but would recognize that different societies face different constraints. So long as an individual takes human dignity to found both positive human rights and obligations, she has reason to act in some way to fulfill those obligations, and coherence requires

15. On the incentive issue, see Minkler 2004; on the social insurance issue, see Sen 2001.
16. Copp 1992. Also see Shue (1988), who argues for a division of labor of duties.
17. Sen (2001) advocates such a procedure to address important policy decisions that do not have an exact answer given by the proper moral considerations.

that the person of integrity does so, absent some other overriding reason (e.g., her own poverty).

Given these conditions, a normative case has been made for the person of integrity to support acts meant to provide and safeguard social security, just wages and working conditions, an adequate standard of living, free public education, and the opportunity to participate in one's culture (human rights, all). The particulars of that support will be determined by the individual's other values and constraints, and also the political and social context in which state action occurs. For a person of integrity, the truth of the existence of the positive obligation is not at issue. And, as a positive matter, surely many recognize this obligation and believe and act accordingly.

Concluding Comment

The logical connections offered here are fairly modest. The goal was to find *sufficient* conditions for a person of integrity to support a particular kind of social contract, human rights. Those conditions are not onerous. Persons of integrity have reason to support human rights if they base their acceptance of the minimalist principle on human dignity. Dignity provides a natural foundation. But the minimalist principle could rest on other philosophies and doctrines; and other principles, philosophies, and doctrines held by the person of integrity could imply different social contracts. Thus I did not attempt to find the *necessary* conditions to support human rights or any other social contract. As discussed, a libertarian who is also a person of integrity has reason to support a less comprehensive social contract, or a human rights one excluding positive rights and duties. In contrast, it is almost self-evident that the person of integrity who holds the principle that "fulfilling human need is good" would have reason to support the full range of human rights. Moreover, persons of integrity who also embrace human rights as a first principle (as in "all human rights are good is true") clearly would be required to match their actions and obligations. That link is direct. Why people would embrace more extensive moral principles is the subject of the next chapter. But one implication of this analysis is that anything that increases moral development is likely to increase both the prevalence of integrity and also support for human rights.

Chapter 9

On the Possibility of Integrity

Having explored what integrity is and how it works, the final question becomes, what factors influence its extent? Specifically, what hinders integrity, and what could promote its development? This chapter investigates those kinds of questions by considering moral training, moral leadership, and integrity-enhancing institutions.

Chapter 3 described the main reasons why a person would fail to act from commitment-integrity. First, and perhaps most important, one may fail to commit to moral principles. That could happen for a number of reasons, but chief among them is the possibility that the person has not achieved the necessary moral maturity. Weakness of the will is the second possibility. In that case, one who has chosen and committed to moral principles does not have the power to override competing desires when choosing actions. Third, one could make an error in judgment when applying their moral principles. A particularly important case occurs if a person mistakenly treats a situation as if it is one of mutual deceit, that is, where lying is both accepted and expected. Fourth, a person could engage in self-deception. Even if literal self-deception is impossible, people will sometimes use psychological tricks to convince themselves that doing what they want is really the same as what is morally required. Finally, and closely related to the last two, is the possibility that a person engages in moral exclusion. That happens, for instance, when one disregards the moral standing of another because of some real or perceived infraction that causes harm. Lying to a liar is the quintessential case. The rest of this chapter considers some factors that might influence all of these failures to act with integrity, and concludes with a discussion of the desirability of increasing the extent of integrity.

9.1. Moral Training and Moral Leadership

Any kind of training involves some kind of instruction and/or exercises. Moral training can vary from religious sermons or talks to classroom lectures on ethics to group discussions of ethical dilemmas. As for moral leadership, first note that leaders set priorities, agendas, and standard operating procedures for subordinates or constituents. Thus, moral leaders give priority to ethical considerations and principles.

To see how moral training and moral leadership can influence decision making, consider the ethical decision-making apparatus of James Rest.[1] He hypothesizes four steps: (1) moral awareness, (2) moral judgment, (3) establishing moral intent, and (4) moral action. Moral awareness means that an agent recognizes the moral nature of a potentially ambiguous situation. Moral judgment refers to making a decision about what is right, a judgment that is determined by one's level of moral reasoning (see the discussion of Piaget and Kohlberg in chapter 3). Establishing moral intent gives priority to what one judges to be right, as opposed to what one wants (assuming they diverge). Although not explicitly recognized by Rest, integrity is particularly important for this step because the existence of integrity increases the likelihood that this step will be fulfilled. If one identifies with and is committed to a moral principle, as is required by commitment-integrity, one is more likely to give priority to that principle. The final step, taking moral action, simply means following intent with actual behavior. The will comes into play here; a weak will may not be able to effectuate acts seen as contrary to one's desires. In fact, a failure in any of the previous three steps decreases the likelihood of moral action.

How then could moral training and leadership contribute to the fulfillment of this four-step process? At the most basic level, moral training and moral leadership expose people to the possibility of applying moral principles to situations. Both types can inform, inspire, and transform. Consider step 1, moral awareness, the crucial first link in the decision chain.[2] Social cognition theory postulates that awareness begins with encoding, which is the representation of external information in one's mind. However, external information is selectively encoded based on people's attention. People typically attend to things that are novel, emotionally interesting, relevant to their goals, or easily accessible to their memories. These attributes, then, facilitate awareness. Thus, moral training and moral leadership can contribute to moral awareness to the extent that they frame situations in moral terms. By framing certain situations in moral language, people come to perceive the moral content of other situations. When an act has more significant moral consequences, the likelihood increases that people will recognize the moral nature of a situation.

1. Rest 1986. Also see Butterfield, Trevino, and Weaver 2000.
2. The following discussion draws from Butterfield, Trevino, and Weaver 2000, 984.

For an interesting example of what the lack of moral training and leadership can do, consider the case of the Ford Pinto. The person in charge of recalls at the time repeatedly voted against recalling the Pinto even when confronted with information that relatively minor rear-end collisions caused serious fires, injuries, and fatalities. He later explained that he did not perceive any moral content in the situation because the corporate "scripts" he was operating from were devoid of moral content. For instance, the corporate language used to describe the Pinto case was a "condition" rather than a "problem," in order to eschew legal culpability. The expression "lighting up" versus "catching fire" or "bursting into flames" was used for the same reason.[3] This kind of euphemistic labeling reduces the chance that a decision maker will recognize the moral nature of a situation. Albert Bandura persuasively argues that euphemisms make it less likely that an agent's moral standards will be activated in the first place. As he writes, "Through convoluted verbiage, destructive conduct is made benign and those who engage in it are relieved of a sense of personal agency."[4] People are more willing to kill innocent civilians in a war if they are called "collateral damage." Perhaps the same kind of thing could be said for lies when they are called "cheap talk."

There is evidence that framing issues in moral terms, the magnitude of consequences, and perceived social consensus can all affect moral awareness in business settings. To study the issue, Kenneth Butterfield, Linda Trevino, and Gary Weaver conducted field experiments that included 291 competitive intelligence practitioners.[5] A relatively new profession, competitive intelligence practitioners gather information about competitors' business practices, strategies, products, and so on in order to aid their own firm's plans. Since the field is still young, norms regarding ethical versus unethical information-gathering techniques are still emerging. Surfing the Internet in search of information is clearly ethical; industrial espionage is not. But there is a large grey area in between.

The researchers presented competitive intelligence practitioners with two different scenarios. In the first, mystery shopping, a person poses as a customer of a competitor's product or service in order to gain information. In the second, a hiring decision, a midlevel manager has to decide whether or not to hire a job candidate who possesses—and is willing to share—valuable information about a competitor's product. Competitive intelligence practitioners were asked to judge either one of the two scenarios by writing down a

3. Butterfield, Trevino, and Weaver 2000, 989.
4. Bandura 1990, 31.
5. Butterfield, Trevino, and Weaver 2000.

list of issues a protagonist would find important. The magnitude of consequences and moral framing effects were captured by manipulating each scenario accordingly, while the perceived social consensus effect was studied with ex post questionnaires. For instance, some competitive intelligence practitioners were asked to comment on scenarios where getting the information right could put a competitor out of business, while others were confronted with the less consequential outcome of denting the competitor's market share. As for issue framing, some scenarios included nonmoral language. For instance, in the hiring decision case sometimes the protagonist proclaimed, "I'm hesitant to bring it up because I know you're busy," but in others he said, "I'm hesitant to bring it up because it might call our *integrity* into question" (emphasis added). Other places in the scenario might use the terms *right* and *wrong* to prompt moral awareness. These manipulations were represented by dichotomous independent variables.

Hierarchical regression analysis found strongly significant effects for both the magnitude of consequences and perceived social consensus variables on moral awareness (the dependent variable) in the pooled sample. The issue-framing variable had a marginally significant effect (i.e., significant at the 10 percent level). However, when the sample was segregated between scenarios, the issue-framing variable was found to be strongly significant in the mystery shopping case but not the hiring decision case. The authors conjecture that that result occurs because the mystery shopping scenario is more morally ambiguous. Also interesting were some of the written responses. For instance, when commenting on the hiring decision scenario, one competitive intelligence practitioner wrote, "One would hope that he (the midlevel manager) has the personal integrity to think twice about hiring someone who would, it seems, be doing something unethical."[6] When referring to the mystery shopping case, another wrote, "Integrity and honesty can never be compromised if anyone is to trust you. This holds true for anyone in your company as well as the competitor's company."[7] Even if this respondent's reasoning was instrumental, clearly his moral awareness had been activated.

Now turn to step 2, the one about moral judgment. Moral judgment involves the determination of what is right, which, in turn, depends on the individual's level of moral reasoning. Lawrence Kohlberg theorized that people progress through stages of moral development, and that each new level of moral development represents a different mode of thinking. People generally prefer to use the highest stage of reasoning available to them, and they move

6. Butterfield, Trevino, and Weaver 2000, 1004.
7. Butterfield, Trevino, and Weaver 2000, 1005.

to higher stages as a result of cognitive disequilibrium. That kind of disequilibrium occurs when the individual is confronted with a situation or dilemma that cannot be adequately addressed, in the person's own mind, with the type of moral thinking they currently use. Empirically, higher stages of moral reasoning are positively correlated with age, education, and the amount of social interaction. As people develop cognitively, they develop through higher stages of moral development.

The evidence strongly indicates that moral training increases moral reasoning.[8] Exposure to higher stages of moral thinking than generally used by an individual can accelerate both the process of cognitive disequilibrium and moral development. For instance, ethics courses have been shown to have a demonstrable effect on undergraduate and medical students' level of moral reasoning. Small group discussions seem most fruitful, perhaps because they involve both instruction and interaction.

While there is less evidence on the effects of moral leadership, some evidence suggests that small groups led by high moral reasoners tend to apply a higher level of moral reasoning to moral dilemmas than those led by lower reasoners.[9] Leaders at a high level of moral reasoning tend to display teaching behavior more so than their lower reasoning counterparts. Moreover, leaders at a high level of moral reasoning tend to display transformational leadership behavior.[10] Transformational leaders inspire, and offer a collective vision based on the group good. Transactional leaders, in contrast, are more controlling of subordinates—who are seen as instrumental ends—and solve problems with individual incentive schemes. As we will see in the next section, we can expect that organizations that institutionalize transactional leadership techniques encourage more self-interested behavior and less integrity-based behavior.

Step 3 involves making a moral decision into a priority. Of course, for the person of integrity the perceived truth of a moral principle provides the reason to make it a priority. Moral training and moral leadership can both inspire people to commit to moral principles. Moral leaders in particular can encourage others by consistently demonstrating commitment themselves. Sometimes committed moral leaders exhibit courage in the face of real danger, or even just the prevailing norms, and that demonstrable willingness to put their conventional interests on the line stimulates others to do the same. By modeling principled behavior, moral leaders teach others to question the

8. For instance, see the metastudy of Rest and Thoma 1986. Also see Page and Bode 1982; Self, Wolinsky, and Baldwin 1989; Trevino 1992.
9. Dukerich et al. 1990.
10. Turner et al. 2002.

desirability of their desires and to reach for something nobler. Moral leaders nudge us to expand the perceived boundaries of our responsibility, to make the welfare of others a priority. Those who choose to live with integrity experience the kind of well-being associated with cognitive equilibrium and coherence of being. Gandhi, Martin Luther King Jr., and Aung San Suu Kyi are obvious exemplars of inspirational moral leadership.

Step 4, moral action, is the culmination of the decision chain. It is the actualization of moral intent. But just because an individual makes moral principles a priority does not mean that she will follow through with the prescribed behavior. As seen in chapter 3, the evidence suggests a positive and significant but modest relationship between the level of one's moral judgment and one's action. Mediating factors include one's strength of will, and perhaps perceived responsibility, as well as those added in this book: failure to choose moral principles, errors in judgment, self-deception, and moral exclusion. All of the latter factors are largely addressed as soon as an individual comes to recognize the decision context as a moral one and makes it a priority. So long as the individual possesses the requisite level of moral maturity, that leaves the will, or, more precisely, the weakness of the will in the face of temptation, as the main obstacle between moral decision and action. As we have seen, given the normal choice constraints, preferences, and the strength of will, the person of integrity acts on a moral principle as long as the will is stronger than the difference in utility from doing what the person wants versus what she thinks is right. As we will see in the next section, incentives could crucially impact this difference.

That the strength of will, preferences, and constraints are exogenous to the individual does not mean they are exogenous to the social system in which the individual operates. Economists are particularly comfortable with the idea of manipulating constraints with conscious institutional design to change behavior (see section 9.2). The question now is whether moral training and moral leadership can either (1) affect the strength of the will, and/or (2) change preferences in such a way that the likelihood of moral acts increases and, if so, how?

For the will, it would mean that moral training and moral leaders could strengthen an individual's power to act on moral principles, in contraposition to her desires. It is not at all clear how moral leadership could do that, and only slightly more clear how moral training could. That kind of moral training might have as its focus exercises that place individuals in slightly tempting situations, and then increase the level of temptation as the individual masters a lower level. The goal would be to change one's power to act, not their moral principles or preferences. If willpower is like a muscle that can be strengthened through exercise, then maybe some kind of moral training makes sense. But that kind of moral exercise would require real situations with real moral consequences. How could one overcome a weakness of lying, for instance, if one doesn't realize the true suffering lying causes? The feasibility of such an exercise as well as its ethical nature is questionable.

We turn now to whether moral training and moral leadership affect preferences. In real life, preferences are at least partially endogenous.[11] Most major institutions in society provide some kind of informational role, but they can also change preferences. That goes for schools, churches, the media, and advertising. What all of this means is that moral training and moral leadership can also form and change preferences. For instance, Martin Luther King Jr. and other African American leaders helped to successfully change the racist preferences of many Americans. The best business leaders induce their workers to move from their most self-centered preferences.[12]

Let me briefly summarize this section on how moral leadership and moral training can impact the four-step moral decision-making process. First, they can increase moral awareness, for instance, by helping to frame situations in moral terms. Second, they can contribute to moral judgment by increasing moral reasoning. Third, moral leadership and moral training can promote moral intent by inspiring people. And finally, they can increase the likelihood of moral action, particularly by changing preferences in such a way that ultimately allows individuals to will those acts most consistent with their principles.

9.2. Institutions

So far the discussion has focused mostly on factors that could influence the individual's propensity to act with moral integrity. We now examine context,

11. See Bowles 1998.

12. In addition, people sometimes misjudge the anticipated welfare from fulfilling their preferences. Indeed, one of the tenets of the economics of happiness literature is that more consumption does not necessarily buy more welfare, quite to the contrary of the social norms and popular views on the topic. Once a certain level of material consumption is achieved, further increases only increase welfare marginally, at best (Oswald 1997; Frank 1997b; also see Comim 2005 for the problem of habituation inherent in subjective evaluations of well-being). So, by their own actions to get more material goods, people consistently demonstrate that they misjudge the relationship between their own preferences and welfare. They overestimate the satisfaction from acquiring more stuff. To the extent that moral training and moral leadership can provide corrective information about the true relationship, it would increase the likelihood that people of given wills and preferences would act on their moral principles. Since people would then be acting based on a more accurate assessment of their own welfare, moral training and moral leadership would increase both their freedom and chance for integrity.

which depends to a large extent on the institutional environment. Institutions can be viewed as constraints on human behavior that shape and facilitate interactions. Douglass North differentiates formal from informal constraints.[13] Formal constraints are consciously determined rules of the game: codified policies, laws, and rights are examples. In contrast, informal constraints arise without collective intention and include things like customs, social norms, conventions, habits, and routines. Taken together, formal and informal constraints add an element of predictability to behavior. For instance, contractors know that when they enter into agreements they obtain certain rights that have been established by contract law. People in the United States drive on the right side of the road and can be reasonably sure that others will do the same. Consumers know that haggling can be expected when they go car shopping but not when they buy toothpaste at the drugstore. Because everyone knows the rules of the game, interactions go smoothly; time and resources needn't be wasted in re-creating the context for each new interaction.

The way institutions can promote integrity involves context and errors in judgment. Without the proper institutional mix, people may mistakenly believe the environment to be governed by mutual deceit, or one where others lack moral standing. The relationship between employers and employees provides an important example. As we saw in chapter 6, many workers do not recognize the employment relationship as one where they agree to put in a good day's work and the employer agrees to provide a good working environment. Survey evidence found that about 20 percent didn't think such agreements exist, while just over 11 percent thought that the agreements exist, but were not important to follow. We might then infer that over 30 percent of American workers do not think that they are under a moral compulsion to provide some agreed-upon effort. They may provide effort for some other reason, like intrinsic motivation, but integrity is not relevant in the workplace context for them. Since it is likely that employers view the employment relationship as one where employees should work hard, the real hazard is that many employees view the situation as one of mutual deceit, like a game with no moral elements or consequences. Or worse, some may view their employers as lacking moral standing, because of acts either real or perceived. In either case, employees may not have reached moral awareness (step 1, as described earlier).

To the extent that these problems do not represent willful deceit on the part of employees, they stem from institutional failure. That employees do not recognize the existence of workplace agreements means that there are not

13. North 1990.

clear, formal employment contracts that spell out the roles and responsibilities of each party. Even less formal policies like periodic performance reviews that spell out expectations would leave little doubt in the employee's mind that she has made a sincere agreement, the violation of which would constitute a lie of moral consequence. In any case, employers can eliminate the possibility of mutual deceit by clearly communicating the existence of morally binding agreements.

Another issue concerns how employees might fail to attribute moral standing to their employers if they perceive that their employers have not lived up to their end of agreements. For instance, an employer could agree to provide a good work environment with advancement possibilities but then fail to deliver. Or the employer could lay off workers contrary to promises, or terminate the pension benefits of retirees. The remaining employees would then view the employer as a liar. One response to liars, though not necessarily the morally justifiable response, is to lie back. Some employees will respond to lying employers by breaking their employment agreements, by withholding effort, say. Employers can reduce that possibility by keeping their agreements.

Similarly, managers and supervisors may break small promises as standard operating procedure. They may promise a bigger office (or cubicle) as reward for a good performance, or certain vacation dates, only to renege for seemingly arbitrary reasons. Such behaviors could characterize the entire workplace, so much so that they become norms. In that case, it is likely that workers would see the context as one of mutual deceit or where others fail to have moral standing, or both. Again, the solution would be for a moral leader (employer) to establish or reestablish honest operating procedures and to model honest behavior herself. Sometimes consciously changing formal constraints (policies and their consequences) can influence informal constraints (norms). Absent that kind of intervention, persons of integrity who would otherwise have reason to keep their agreements may fail to do so.

In chapter 6, I mentioned the systematic evidence in Yochi Cohen-Charash and Paul Spector's meta-analysis on the role of fairness in organizations. A key finding of that study was that work performance was related to procedural fairness in organizations. That finding might result because it is more difficult for employees to rationalize mutual deceit with organizations seen as fair.

For additional evidence, consider the role of cultural honesty in organizations examined by psychologist Aleza Greene in his study of worker attitudes in two Houston area grocery chains. Survey respondents were asked about their organization's culture of honesty with thirteen statements like "In this organization, ethics are just as important as profits" and "I believe top management is less honest than the rest of the employees." To assess employee honesty, respondents were asked about their own (and other employees') behaviors with questions of how often they "goofed off," took home money or merchandise, took long lunches, and the like. The study also included demographic variables of the 288 respondents, as well as measures of job satisfaction and organizational commitment. Regression analysis indicates that respondents reported participating in less dishonest behavior the more they reported greater job satisfaction, commitment to their organization, and cultural honesty. Without naming it as such, Greene attributes these results to the role of mutual deceit when he writes, "When employees believe dishonesty is part of their every day work life, when they feel it is part of the philosophy of the organization, and when they can confirm this feeling with evidence of their co-workers engaging in dishonest behavior, they are more likely to behave dishonestly themselves. Perhaps they feel there is nothing wrong with being dishonest because everyone else does it"[14]—that is, when dishonesty is the accepted rule of the game.

The institutional structure of work itself may contribute to the possibility of moral decision making.[15] The locus of control is one important element of the way work is structured. If work is organized hierarchically, subordinates retain little decision-making power over their assigned tasks. The selection of work tasks, the way in which they are performed, and the ultimate responsibility for a project's overall performance all rest with others up the chain of command. The purported advantages of hierarchical work structures include harnessing the benefits of specialization and the facilitation of monitoring worker performance.[16] The potential costs include retarding moral judgments and the lower likelihood that workers will honor their agreements because workers in hierarchies have limited opportunities for interactive role playing. They are also more likely to attribute the responsibility for the project's success to others in the chain. In contrast, more participatory work structures facilitate interactions where workers must consider others' points of view—their problems and challenges, and how their actual decisions could affect others. Moral development theorists identify role playing of this type, in both work and educational settings, as an important contributor that increases moral judgment.[17]

14. Greene 1999, 48.

15. See especially Trevino 1992.

16. Williamson 1975.

17. Trevino 1992. Trevino further suggests that some evidence shows, particularly from social psychology, that the diffusion of responsibility can mediate between moral judgment and moral action. For instance, a bystander to an emergency is less likely to act on a moral judgment if he is one of many bystanders—presumably because he views his individual responsibility as diluted. Trevino

Moreover, the evidence suggests that organizations with participatory practices are more likely to be seen as procedurally fair, itself a significant correlate of positive worker performance. In their meta-analysis on fairness, Cohen-Charash and Spector find a strong relationship between procedural fairness and "voice" (mean correlation coefficient of .52 in six field studies with 708 participants; mean correlation of .38 in 15 laboratory experiments with 2,037 participants).[18] Organizations that allow workers to express their views can increase their moral standing with workers.

A final, very important, way that institutions can affect moral decision making is through the constraints individuals face. Most fundamentally, the more an "immoral" decision costs, the less likely it will occur. Based on standard economic analysis, for a given level of moral judgment (especially in Kohlberg's first four stages), an individual is more likely to *act* morally if the benefits exceed the costs of doing so. The consequences of any decision can be manipulated through conscious institutional design, and doing so can be seen as a form of mediating between moral judgment and moral decision. At least that is the way psychologists would frame it. For example, suppose a worker has made a judgment that to break an agreement and to shirk would be wrong, but that the penalties for doing so would be slight and the rewards great. Perhaps managers monitor infrequently, and even when they do catch a shirker, they don't do much in the way of punishment. And maybe the worker doesn't care much about the firm or his co-workers. In such a case we could pretty much assume that the worker will shirk. The institutional setting encourages it because the worker is little constrained.

Consider another example. Now suppose that the workplace is very competitive. Individuals compete directly with one another for promotions and other benefits, and the firm's management emphasizes productivity, profits, and beating the competition. Those who contribute to this mission succeed, those who don't are fired. A worker confronted with a moral decision, say betraying the confidence of a colleague in order to advance her own career (the colleague is a drug user), may act against her moral judgment precisely because the benefits of doing so exceed the costs in this company.

The reasoning for workers of integrity is somewhat different. If a worker has committed to the principle of not lying, she has reason not to break an

---

also uses an insight from cultural anthropology—that individuals adopt different roles in different contexts, to suggest that the roles managers have to play in organizations may actually retard their level of moral judgment. The idea is that the temptations to choose lower-level moral acts, ones aligned with the expectations of the firm, are too great even if the manager reasons at higher levels in other roles.

18. Cohen-Charash and Spector 2001, table 2, 294.

agreement to work hard or to betray the confidence of a colleague. Further, if she has a sufficiently strong will, it would not matter how the organization has structured the costs and benefits of deception, because the external constraint is not relevant. If the worker's will is strong enough to override the externally determined benefits of deception, she does not lie. For similarly committed workers but with a weaker will, the constraint does matter. If the benefits of deception greatly exceed the costs, then the worker may fail to follow her moral principle because the strength of her will is insufficient to power the moral act. Therefore, organizations can increase the likelihood of moral behavior in all types of workers (except those workers of integrity with strong will, for whom moral behavior is already guaranteed) if it structures its reward system accordingly. To do so, they could adopt policies that encourage honest behavior. Lying would be punished, with honest behavior the expected norm, and possibly rewarded.

Such policies are important because some evidence suggests that misrepresentation is more likely the higher are the incentives to misrepresent. Ann Tenbrunsel conducted a controlled experiment with business students in order to test the effects of changes in the incentive to misrepresent information in a negotiation-type setting.[19] Two students were partnered in the context of a firm that was dissolving. The value of the firm that each student received depended in part on information provided by the student to an arbitrator in charge of deciding shares. The incentive to misrepresent was manipulated by announcing that prizes would be awarded to those students receiving the highest shares from the arbitrator. Students in the high-incentive category could win a hundred dollars, compared to a prize of one dollar for those in the low-incentive category. Among students in the high-incentive condition, 69.4 percent misrepresented their contribution to the firm, (statistically) significantly more than the 41 percent of those who misrepresented in the low-incentive condition. Tenbrunsel interprets this evidence to suggest that an agent's own moral code and also incentives both play a role in ethical dilemmas.

The efficiency wage literature also focuses on incentives, but through the lens of fairness. The idea is that a firm that pays a wage premium can expect higher contributions from its work force because should workers lose their jobs they would have to take inferior alternatives (worse jobs elsewhere). With efficiency wages, workers are more likely to perceive their wages as fair, which in turn allows firms to reduce their monitoring and turnover costs.[20]

19. Tenbrunsel 1998.

20. See, for instance, Akerlof 1984; Shapiro and Stiglitz 1984. Excessive monitoring can also reduce effort if it crowds out intrinsic motivations (as discussed in chapter 6, this volume).

David Levine provides some interesting, relevant evidence for the idea.[21] Using subjective and objective data from firms in both the United States (47 plants with 2,740 workers) and Japan (34 plants with 1,715 workers), he finds that workers with high wages are more likely to report higher job satisfaction and commitment to their firms. For instance, in both countries workers with high wages were less likely to report that "deciding to work for this company was a mistake." Moreover, in the United States those with high wages were more likely to report "I'm willing to work harder than I have to for this company."[22] Overall, in the United States 15 of the 16 performance measures have the sign predicted by the efficiency wage literature (12 of which are statistically significant), while for the Japanese firms 11 of the 12 performance measures used had the predicted sign (but only 4 are statistically significant). Going back to the context here, the use of an efficiency wage surely signals that an employer does not view the employment relationship as one of mutual deceit and possesses a costly punishment for those employees who think otherwise. If employers recognized their relationship with their employees as a moral one, they could devise other institutional designs to discourage unethical behaviors and to promote ethical ones.

9.3. Conclusion

We have seen that moral training, moral leadership, and institutional design can help promote acts from integrity. Even if one accepts that these things might enhance integrity, the critic may question the desirability of doing so. Few would disagree that the more agreements that are kept the better; certainly such a cooperative state would facilitate exchange and reduce enforcement costs. Similarly, few would argue that lying in general is right or desirable. But some might question the cost of promoting integrity. For instance, in questioning the desirability of moral education, especially as a way of promoting voluntary redistributions from the well-off to the less well-off, Ken Binmore made these observations.

> Currently, the gap between the aspirations of our moral pundits and their success in implementing their aspirations is spectacularly wide. This is perhaps because, in order to qualify as a moral pundit, one must abandon all attempts to be realistic about the nature of human nature.[23]

21. Levine 1991.
22. The regression coefficients for these results are also statistically significant.
23. Binmore 1994, 135.

A few lines down, he asks, "if we could effectively brainwash all our children to pursue some invented common good, should we do so?" His answer is no, because a society of freethinkers, some of whom are opportunists, is better than a society of virtuous zealots who are not free.[24]

There are two points to address here. First, Binmore (and many others) offer a conception of human nature that is generally unfavorable. The argument is always the same: people can't be counted on to do such and such good thing because it is against their greedy nature, which is to say, human nature. Such commentators do not seem to be aware of the moral development literature in psychology. Still, it is obviously true that humans possess greed. Buddhists argue that it is greed (along with hatred and ignorance) that is responsible for all human suffering. But it is also true that humans care, love, show tremendous kindness and compassion, and do commit to moral principles. Are those traits not part of human nature? It seems more reasonable to abandon the good/bad dualisms and accept that the human condition allows all possibilities. Like muscles, the question is which ones should we strengthen through exercise.

The question about brainwashing children when it comes to not lying is a serious query. To what extent should we consciously train others not to lie?[25] There are two responses. First, we already do teach "lying is wrong" in most major institutions in society, from families, to school, to church, to work, to our legal system, even if some of the moral justifications are probably not well known. Second, this work suggests that students should be exposed to all ethical views as a regular part of their educational programs. That curriculum would touch on lying but go much further to include topics like moral-political theories on redistribution. While there is reason to be concerned about any kind of indoctrination, like some advertising, a proper education exposes students to different ideas.[26] Their very freedom is actualized when they choose one idea over another.

---

24. Since Binmore does not believe in a free will, it is not clear what he means by "free thinkers."

25. Unlike Binmore, Robert Frank (1988, 248–53) has argued for teaching commonly accepted moral values, including not lying. Doing so, he suggests, would increase the likelihood that children would develop emotional commitments to behave morally.

26. Persuasive advertising is predicated upon getting consumers to respond to a perceived ego deficiency, latent fear, or emotional attachment. It seeks to keep the reasons for its attraction unavailable to the consumer. While it is true that we may never know our full motivations, moral indoctrination of that type is unacceptable because integrity, at least, is based on a free, if only weak, will. Conscious attempts to impinge on that freedom are thus contrary to the very foundations of integrity. Moreover, any moral education that insists that Kant is right and Utilitarians are wrong would be just as objectionable as one that teaches Cervantes is better than Shakespeare, or that one view of history or politics or economics is right and all others are wrong.

Chapter 10

Conclusion

I have argued that integrity exists, and that it is economically meaningful. In this concluding chapter I will briefly summarize some of the main points, suggest future research avenues, and discuss how integrity might be placed in or compared with other virtues. The last point means to address those who value different ethical systems, like the feminist notion of an ethic of care or Aristotelian virtue ethics. Throughout the book I have tried to address potential criticisms from mainstream economists. I conclude by addressing the possible concerns of an audience predisposed to be more sympathetic.

Two different kinds of integrity have been offered. First, preference-integrity exists when one has a strong preference for honesty. That preference overrides other material preferences or contingent interests so that the person of preference-integrity has reason to behave honestly, even at material cost. This kind of person uses what philosophers call externalist reasons. The preference for honesty is the motivating reason; there is no provision for the individual of preference-integrity to evaluate her preference, and thus no link between such an evaluation and her motivation to act. So it is for all instrumentally rational behavior.

Apart from explaining a lot of real-life behavior, perhaps the best thing about preference-integrity is that it fits nicely into the usual utility-maximizing framework of economics. No new techniques are needed, just a new preference. In particular, chapter 4 illustrates in a simple game-theoretic framework how individuals of varying intensities of honesty could be expected to behave in a generic economic agreement with the possibility of exit. Under reasonable assumptions, all agents make a promise in stage 1 and then either lie with certainty in stage 2, keep their promise with certainty, or, if their preference for honesty is in the middle range, behave contingently. For those who keep their word, it is their preference for honesty rather than anticipated reciprocity that primarily drives their behavior. Thus, the analysis differs from virtually all of those in the literature. Nevertheless, nothing about preference-integrity is inconsistent with the literature, and in particular, it seems that preference-integrity could easily become the focus of evolutionary game-theoretic analyses.

The biggest problem with preference-integrity is that it does not and cannot include coherence, a notion so central to both common understandings of integrity and philosophers' accounts. Coherence requires consistency among chosen principles, motivation and principle, and principle and action. As I have said throughout, there is nothing in preference-integrity that would eliminate the possibility of lying to a left-handed person, but not to a right-handed person, because there is no mechanism to assure consistent principles. Instead, preferences are assumed to be exogenously given to the individual. Other problems with preference-integrity are that it is reductionist, self-referential, instrumental, and deterministic. Like any utility-based framework, that means all dispositions, like honesty, can be thought of as preferences, that individuals only take actions to fulfill their own preferences, and since those preferences are exogenous to the individual, there is no provision for conscious reflection or a free will.

Commitment-integrity, the second kind of integrity, overcomes those problems. Commitment-integrity exists when an individual consciously chooses principles, commits to those principles, and wills acts accordingly. There must be coherence as described above. If all of these conditions hold, we can say that the person has an internalist reason to act. That is, the perceived truth of her principles provides the reason to act, quite independent of any competing (or complementary) preferences. Thus commitment-integrity is not reductionist, self-referential, instrumental, or deterministic. The person of commitment-integrity freely chooses to act according to those principles she has freely committed to. Many causes could conspire to explain why one might not act with commitment-integrity. Chief among them are a failure to choose principles, judgment errors, self-deception, moral exclusion, and weakness of will. The first four are especially problematic if the relevant contexts for action are not framed in a moral way (e.g., "everyone lies in this department"); the last is especially problematic when there are strong competing desires ("I know I shouldn't lie, but I really want the time off that lying will get me").

Even if commitment-integrity is more descriptively accurate for many individuals in many types of agreements, its biggest problem is the difficulty of modeling it. I sketched a framework in chapter 3, but that only highlighted the problem of preexisting determinants. Economists embrace utility theory at least partly because, given exogenously determined preferences, prices, and initial endowments, precise solutions can often be derived in problems of choice. In contrast, by its very nature, commitment-integrity does not offer the same kind of determinacy because commitments to principles are not predetermined by anything else. That's what makes the will free. Nevertheless, once commitments are chosen (exogenous for the modeler, but not the individual being modeled), hypotheses can be derived and tested. Both the theoretical framework and empirical tests will require new techniques, and that cost might dissuade those who embrace methodological simplicity. That view itself has a cost because of the realism sacrificed, but there is no question that methodological realism is also costly.

By adhering to the minimalist moral principle of "lying is wrong" and by focusing on the normative requirement of coherence, implications obvious and not so obvious were generated in different kinds of agreements. Most obviously, the existence of integrity reduces different kinds of shirking, by politicians and employees, for instance, because to shirk is to lie. Perhaps not so obvious are some of the recommended solutions. If firms want to prevent shirking, they should offer clear, fair employment agreements and then act fairly themselves. Moreover, it turns out that participatory work schemes can increase moral awareness and moral development, thereby increasing the chances that workers would become workers of integrity. Such recommendations constitute a stark contrast to those of the main theories of the firm, which instead recommend monitoring, incentive contracts, and hierarchy. Even so, clear, fair agreements might be insufficient to induce knowledge contributions by workers. Instead, effort might be directed toward creating interesting work conditions that act on intrinsic motivations.

The normative requirement of coherence also leads to some not so obvious implications. For instance, even if we stick with the minimalist moral principle, a person of integrity has reason to support a social contract like human rights, so long as the reason such a person embraces that principle is to minimize harm. But the focus on coherence also reveals another problem for the person of integrity. By expanding the scope of principles that a person of integrity might commit to, as when we include religious principles (the topic of chapter 7), we see that time constraints might necessitate a certain kind of incoherence. No matter the sincerity of intent, it might be quite impossible to commit to being simultaneously a faithful religious practitioner, a good mother, a good employee, a good friend, and a good citizen. There simply might not be enough time to meet the demands of all of those chosen identities. We know what happened to Don Quixote when he tried to always do right.

One can only hope that the novelty of these implications will convince researchers about the rewards of investigating integrity further. The next step would be to refine the theoretical modeling of integrity. Since preference-integrity uses utility theory, it should be fairly straightforward to deepen and extend that analysis. For instance, we could see what happens when agents are differentially endowed with preference-integrity in social dilemmas over time. Under some restrictive conditions, Tom Miceli and I found that switching behavior can occur, for instance, when a person who lied in the last period tells the truth in the next period. But how that might happen in a more general framework needs further investigation.[1] Furthermore, how a preference for honesty itself might change over time could be the topic of evolutionary game-theoretic analyses. A full analysis would require the inclusion of the possibility of differential harm from lying since the evidence shows that people are less likely to lie when they perceive that their lies cause harm.

Commitment-integrity might prove a tougher nut. While we cannot include the predeterminants of commitments to principles in our models, nothing precludes including influences. Behavioral economists have already been looking at how framing and contexts matter for decision making. That same strategy could be applied to the factors mentioned here for the person of integrity, namely, the failure to choose principles, judgment errors, self-deception, moral exclusion, and weakness of will. As an example, a fuller analysis could include the factors that influence an individual to exclude another from their principled decision making, thereby relegating that other to a preference instead. In other words, why would Martha not do what she thinks is right when referring to John (but not Fred) and instead do as she wants. As for the will, a fuller analysis might include factors that could change its strength. For instance, we might explore the possibility of a weakening will as one takes tempting actions versus a strengthening one as one practices restraint.

There are two empirical avenues that need further exploration. First and foremost, we need to map out the prevalence of integrity, especially with respect to the minimalist principle because that would be most relevant for economic agreements. Ample experimental evidence demonstrates that promise making reduces the incidence of noncooperation, while other experimental evidence shows that lying decreases with perceived harm. But those are results from contrived experimental settings. Survey evidence suggests that workers won't break agreements and shirk if they promised not to. But surveys, for all of their value, don't measure what people actually do. Casual observation demonstrates that people often keep their agreements even when they could cheat, but we don't have an exact handle on how often that happens. Part of the reason is probably because economists and other social scientists have yet

1. Minkler and Miceli 2004.

to think about how to measure honest behavior, perhaps because we don't model people as honest. That can't be the whole reason, however, because there have been almost no attempts to measure the extent of actual dishonest behavior in contractual settings, even though that's what we assume. So perhaps the biggest reason we haven't tried in earnest to estimate either honest or dishonest behavior is because it is just difficult to do. But it is important.

The second empirical issue concerns measuring a given individual's integrity. Of course revealed preference techniques won't work. What's needed instead is something more akin to Lawrence Kohlberg's interviewing techniques. In order to find out about a person's commitments to principles versus their preferences, say, they will have to be asked probing, precise, replicable questions. Once the degree of integrity is measured, experimental games could be designed to determine things like strength of will, the importance of different factors behind the propensity to exclude others from principled decision making, and so on. As mentioned in chapter 3, to not investigate the role of integrity in contexts of agreements risks omitting an important behavioral consideration from our current analyses.

I have repeatedly tried to defend the necessity of including integrity in economic analyses, mostly by appealing to methodological realism. In these last few pages, I would like to respond to those who might criticize this account on the opposite grounds, namely, that including integrity in economic analyses still does not go far enough. These critics might argue that what I have offered is still incomplete because it does not include important dispositions like emotions, caring, and other virtues. That objection could represent the views of feminist economists, among others.

Feminist economists typically eschew principle-based moralizing. That perspective is associated with a patriarchic, male-gendered orientation, and is too abstract. Instead, focus is placed more on the female-gendered attribute of caring, by acknowledging the needs of others. Caring occurs in real relationships, between real people, as in relationships among family members. From this perspective, an ethic of care has emerged that emphasizes the needs of others, the responsibility and competence of caregivers, and also the responsibilities of the care receiver (e.g., communicating their needs).[2] This ethic has its source in the emotions, because it is our sympathies for another's plight (unmet needs) that provides the motivation for our caregiving practices. Feminist economists have used these ideas to analyze caring labor (e.g., health care and child care provision) and how it's undervalued in an economy dom-

2. See, for instance, Fisher and Tronto 1990; Tronto 1993.

inated by male-gendered values.[3] For too long there has been a perception that an activity is of value only if it is exchanged for a price on the market.

Virginia Held has gone further to suggest that we might use the caring typified by an archetypical mothering person as a conceptual model for myriad human relationships, including even the social contract. The use of "this approach suggests that just as relations between persons within the family should be based on concern and caring, rather than on egoistic or nontuistic contracts, so various relations in the wider society should be characterized by more care and concern and openness and trust and human feeling than are the contractual bargains that have developed so far in political and economic life, or even aspired to in contractarian prescriptions. Then, the household instead of the marketplace may provide a model for society."[4] Her analysis explicitly privileges care over abstract moral principles.

Irene van Staveren is more inclusive.[5] She develops a framework that includes a variety of ethical capabilities (including commitment, emotion, deliberation, and interaction) and applies them to three different domains: freedom, justice, and care. The result is that individuals need to balance many values in order to successfully traverse all different kinds of human relationships.[6] Interestingly, van Staveren borrows from Aristotelian virtue ethics to show how different values can be achieved. Aristotle did not prescribe principles of justice; rather for him the good lies in attaining virtues. Virtues result from trial and error, the mean between excess and deficiency. For van Staveren that signifies that a value like care is a mean between others and can be found by experimenting with values in the other domains, like autonomy in the domain of freedom and dependence in the domain of justice.

I would respond to a presumed critique from feminists in a couple of ways. First, emotions (e.g., guilt, indignation) are often necessary to signal the need for moral action and to sustain it. At some level, caring is necessary to propel one not to harm others. Still, these kinds of desires to act morally may

3. See, for instance, Folbre 1995; Nelson 1999.

4. Held 1990, 294.

5. Van Staveren 2001.

6. To illustrate the complexity of the idea, consider the following summary passage. "As a consequence, in order to be rational, economic actors need to invest in all the virtues, that is, in *all* ethical capabilities in *each* of the domains. They need to develop value *commitments* to freedom, justice, and care with their respective virtues. They need to acquire the capability to experience *emotions* belonging to each of these domains, such as pride (freedom), rightness (justice), and affection (care). They need to develop capabilities to *deliberate,* that is, to make choices (freedom), to agree on a legitimate distribution (justice), and to evaluate in relationship with other people's contingent needs (care). Finally, economic actors need to learn to *interact* with each other, that is, to compete in exchange (freedom), to follow agreed rules (justice), and to share what they are able to give (care)" (van Staveren 2001, 150–51, emphasis in original).

themselves be the product of the reflection on and acceptance of moral principles, as argued in chapter 3. On this account, it is the perceived truth of moral principles that provides the most primitive reason for moral action.

That's important because sometimes one may not particularly *feel* like acting morally. If I am bored or angry, I may not feel like telling you the truth. If I don't care about you, I may not feel the need to tell you the truth. But it's just not clear why regard for you should depend upon my emotional state. Emotions are often unreliable. One moment our emotions are fellow-feeling, yet in the very next anger promotes lashing out. In contrast, moral principles like "lying is wrong" are universal, and it is that universality that assures everyone gets equal regard.

The issue of virtue, and especially Aristotle's virtue ethics, is an interesting one. Both the philosophical and psychological bases for commitment-integrity are fairly Platonic in the sense that it is an individual's quest for truth that compels her to be a person of integrity. In contrast, virtue ethics counsel individuals to develop certain characteristics like patience, courage, and truthfulness, rather than to fruitlessly try to find the right answers to moral problems. Nevertheless, the two approaches need not be in conflict. Some philosophers tout integrity as a virtue because it requires a self that is integrated and whole.[7] Philosopher Mark Halfon considers the relationship between integrity and Aristotle's virtue ethics directly.[8] He believes that integrity is a necessary virtue among many for the virtuous person—it has contributive value. That seems about right to me; moral integrity could be considered a virtue, but certainly not the only one nor even the most admirable one.

As pointed out by Irene van Staveren, there are many virtues worthy of consideration in economic analyses. Her own framework includes an almost dizzying array. The problem of course is that by being so inclusive one risks losing any semblance of tractability. In trying to be sensitive to the critique of methodological simplicity, I have therefore focused mostly on the one minimalist moral principle of "lying is wrong." That keeps the analysis tractable and leads to fairly precise implications. It also seems to target the virtue/value/principle most relevant for the contexts I consider, namely, agreements. Others have focused on altruism and fairness, and those kinds of virtues are appropriate in instances of tipping, helping strangers in distress, contributing to public goods, and sharing windfall gains. Those kinds of sentiments seem less relevant when agreements, explicit or implicit, are under consideration.

7. See Halfon 1989, 50–51.
8. Halfon 1989, chapter 11 ("Aristotle and the Contributive Value of Integrity"). Halfon's version of integrity requires a commitment to the moral perspective of "doing what's best" rather than to any specific moral principles.

Contractual parties often do not, and need not, have any particular affinity for one another beyond an aversion against lying to one another. For that reason, I intentionally excluded certain relationships from the analysis that have sometimes been treated as if they were contractual, like marriages and intrafamily distributions. Omitting sentiments like care in those instances surely misses a central feature of those relationships.

My purpose in examining integrity in the agreement setting has certainly been one of trying to explain how and why real people behave, rather than how to best behave. I would not claim integrity to be the highest virtue. Perhaps the biggest reason for that is that integrity requires one to make *identity*-conferring commitments. Identity is crucial. But while identity considerations seem to be the focus of a lot of scholarly and political attention, as a normative matter, by creating and holding to identities, individuals must create "others," other people ("those" people), as well as other principles ("those" principles). So that kind of dualism holds even for persons of integrity. Once there are others, there is the possibility, if not necessity, of self-conscious action and harm. In contrast, if it were possible to get beyond identity of any sort, true compassion would become possible. This is the compassion, or the kindness not propelled by "I" and "other," that Buddhists refer to. Perhaps the highest virtue, compassion is certainly more virtuous than the type of care normally considered because it does not depend on any specific relationship with any specific other. But until *that* world emerges, virtues like care and integrity both seem worthy because each reduces suffering in *this* world.

Bibliography

Adler, Moshe. 1992. "The Quality Guaranteeing Price with Market Anonymity." *International Journal of Game Theory* 21: 313–23.

Akerlof, George A. 1984. "Gift Exchange and Efficiency Wage Theory: Four Views." *American Economic Review* 74 (2):79–83.

Akerlof, George A., and R. E. Kranston. 2000. "Economics and Identity." *Quarterly Journal of Economics* 105:715–53.

Akerlof, George A., and Rachel E. Kranston. 2005. "Identity and the Economics of Organization." *Journal of Economic Perspectives* 19:9–32.

Alchian, Armen, and Harold Demsetz. 1972. "Production, Information Costs, and Economic Organization." *American Economic Review* 62:777–95.

Anderson, Gary. 1988. "Mr. Smith and the Preachers: The Economics of Religion in the Wealth of Nations." *Journal of Political Economy* 96:1066–88.

Baier, Annette. 1990. "Why Honesty Is a Hard Virtue." In *Identity, Character, and Morality,* ed. O. Flanagan and A. Rorty. Cambridge: MIT Press.

Bandura, Albert. 1990. "Selective Activation and Disengagement of Moral Control." *Journal of Social Issues* 46:27–46.

Bandura, Albert. 1991. "Social Cognitive Theory of Moral Thought and Action." In *Handbook of Moral Behavior and Development,* ed. W. Kurtines and J. Gerwitz, vol. 1, *Theory.* Hillsdale, NJ: Lawrence Erlbaum.

Basu, Kaushik. 2006. "Identity, Trust, and Altruism: Sociological Clues to Economic Development." Manuscript, Department of Economics, Cornell University.

Bechara, Antoine, and Antonio Damasio. 2005. "The Somatic Marker Hypothesis: A Neural Theory of Economic Decision." *Games and Economic Behavior* 52:336–72.

Beck, Lewis. 1960. *A Commentary on Kant's Critique of Practical Reason.* Chicago: University of Chicago Press.

Beetham, David. 1995. "What Future for Economic and Social Rights?" *Political Studies* 43:41–60.

Bender, Bruce, and John Lott. 1996. "Legislator Voting and Shirking: A Critical Review of the Literature." *Public Choice* 87:67–100.

Bikchandani, Sushil, David Hirshleifer, and Ivo Welsh. 1992. "A Theory of Fads, Fashion, Custom, and Cultural Change as Informational Cascades." *Journal of Political Economy* 100:992–1026.

Binmore, Ken. 1994. *Game Theory and the Social Contract.* Vol. 1, *Playing Fair.* Cambridge: MIT Press.

Binmore, Ken. 1998. *Game Theory and the Social Contract.* Vol. 2, *Just Playing.* Cambridge: MIT Press.

Binmore, Ken, and Larry Samuelson. 1992. "Evolutionary Stability in Repeated Games Played by Finite Automata." *Journal of Economic Theory* 57:278–305.

Blasi, Augusto. 1980. "Bridging Moral Cognition and Moral Action: A Critical Review of the Literature." *Psychological Bulletin* 88:1–45.

Blasi, Augusto. 1983. "Moral Cognition and Moral Action: A Theoretical Perspective." *Developmental Review* 3:178–210.

Blustein, Jeffrey. 1991. *Care and Commitment: Taking the Personal Point of View.* New York: Oxford University Press.

Boden, Margaret. 1980. *Jean Piaget.* New York: Viking Press.

Bok, Sissela. 1978. *Lying: Moral Choice in Public and Private Life.* New York: Pantheon.

Bowles, Samuel. 1998. "Endogenous Preferences: The Cultural Consequences of Markets and Other Economic Institutions." *Journal of Economic Literature* 36:75–111.

Boyd, Robert, and Peter Richerson. 1990. "Culture and Cooperation." In *Beyond Self-Interest,* ed. J. Mansbridge. Chicago: University of Chicago Press.

Brennan, Timothy. 1989. "A Methodological Assessment of Multiple Utility Frameworks." *Economics and Philosophy* 5:189–208.

Brennan, Timothy. 1993. "The Futility of Multiple Utility." *Economics and Philosophy* 9:155–64.

Buber, Martin. 1958. *I and Thou.* New York: Charles Scribner's Sons.

Butterfield, Kenneth, Linda Trevino, and Gary Weaver. 2000. "Moral Awareness in Business Organizations: Influences of Issue Related and Social Context Factors." *Human Relations* 53:981–1018.

Caporael, Linda, Robyn Dawes, John Orbell, and Alphons van de Kragt. 1989. "Selfishness Examined: Cooperation in the Absence of Egoistic Incentives." *Behavioral and Brain Sciences* 4:683–98.

Coase, Ronald. 1937. "The Nature of the Firm." *Economica* 4:386–405.

Cohen, Jonathan. 2005. "The Vulcanization of the Human Brain: A Neural Perspective on Interactions between Cognition and Emotion." *Journal of Economic Perspectives* 19 (4): 3–24.

Cohen-Charash, Yochi, and Paul Spector. 2001. "The Role of Justice in Organizations: A Meta-Analysis." *Organizational Behavior and Human Decision Processes* 86 (2): 278–321.

Colby, Anne, and Lawrence Kohlberg. 1987. *The Measurement of Moral Judgement.* Vol. 1. Cambridge: Cambridge University Press.

Comim, Flavio. 2005. "Capabilities and Happiness: Potential Synergies." *Review of Social Economy* 63:161–76.

Conlisk, John. 1996. "Why Bounded Rationality?" *Journal of Economic Literature* 34:669–700.

Copp, David. 1992. "A Right to an Adequate Standard of Living: Justice, Autonomy, and the Basic Needs." *Social Philosophy and Policy* 9:231–61.

Cosgel, Metin, and Lanse Minkler. 2004a. "Rationality, Integrity, and Religious Behavior." *Journal of Socio-Economics* 33:329–41.

Cosgel, Metin, and Lanse Minkler. 2004b. "Religious Identity and Consumption." *Review of Social Economy* 62:339–50.

Cosmides, Leda, and John Tooby. 1994. "Better than Rational: Evolutionary Psychology and the Invisible Hand." *American Economic Review* 84 (2): 327–32.

Darwall, Stephen. 1983. *Impartial Reason.* Ithaca: Cornell University Press.

Darwall, Stephen. 1997. "Reasons, Motives, and the Demands of Morality: An Introduction." In *Moral Discourse and Practice: Some Philosophical Approaches,* ed. S. Darwall, A. Gibbard, and P. Railton. New York: Oxford University Press.

Davidson, Donald. 1963. "Actions, Reasons, and Causes." *Journal of Philosophy* 60:685–700.

Davis, D., and C. Holt. 1993. *Experimental Economics.* Princeton: Princeton University Press.

Davis, John. 2003. *Theory of the Individual in Economics.* New York: Routledge.

Dawes, Robyn, J. McTavish, and H. Shaklee. 1977. "Behavior, Communication, and Assumptions about Other People's Behavior in Commons Dilemma Situations." *Journal of Personality and Social Psychology* 35:1–11.

DePaulo, Bella, Deborah Kashy, Susan Kirkendol, Melissa Wyler, and Jennifer Epstein. 1996. "Lying in Everyday Life." *Journal of Personality and Social Psychology* 70:979–95.

Dow, Gregory. 2003. *Governing the Firm: Workers' Control in Theory and Practice.* Cambridge: Cambridge University Press.

Dowell, Richard, Robert Goldfarb, and William Griffith. 1998. "Economic Man as a Moral Individual." *Economic Inquiry* 36:645–53.

Dukerich, Janet, Mary Nichols, Dawn Elm, and David Vollrath. 1990. "Moral Reasoning in Groups: Leaders Make a Difference." *Human Relations* 43:473–93.

Eaton, Curtis, and William White. 1991. "The Distribution of Wealth and the Efficiency of Institutions." *Economic Inquiry* 29:336–50.

Elster, Jon. 1998. "Emotions and Economic Theory." *Journal of Economic Literature* 36:47–74.

Endler, Norman, Philippe Rushton, and Henry Roediger. 1978. "Productivity and Scholarly Impact." *American Psychologist* 33:1064–82.

Etzioni, Amitai. 1986. "The Case for a Multiple-Utility Conception." *Economics and Philosophy* 2:159–83.

Etzioni, Amitai. 1988. *The Moral Dimension: Towards a New Economics.* New York: Free Press.

Falk, W. D. 1947–48. "Ought and Motivation." *Proceedings of the Aristotelian Society* 48:111–38.

Fehr, Ernst, and Armin Falk. 2002. "Psychological Foundations of Incentives." *European Economic Review* 46:687–724.

Fehr, Ernst, and Simon Gächter. 2000a. "Cooperation and Punishment in Public Goods Experiments." *American Economic Review* 90:980–94.

Fehr, Ernst, and Simon Gächter. 2000b. "Fairness and Retaliation: The Economics of Reciprocity." *Journal of Economic Perspectives* 14:159–81.

Fehr, Ernst, and Klaus Schmidt. 1999. "A Theory of Fairness, Competition, and Cooperation." *Quarterly Journal of Economics* 114:817–68.

Feinberg, Joel. 1970. "The Nature and Value of Rights." *Journal of Value Inquiry* 4:243–51.

Fisher, Bernice, and Jane Tronto. 1990. "Toward a Feminist Theory of Caring." In *Circles of Care,* ed. E. Abel and M. Nelson, 35–62. Albany: State University of New York Press.

Folbre, Nancy. 1995. "Holding Hands at Midnight: The Paradox of Caring Labour." *Feminist Economics* 1:73–92.

Foot, Philippa. 1972. "Morality as a System of Hypothetical Imperatives." *Philosophical Review* 81:305–16. Reprinted in *Moral Discourse and Practice: Some Philosophical Approaches,* ed. S. Darwall, A. Gibbard, and P. Railton. New York: Oxford University Press, 1997.

Frank, Robert. 1987. "If *Homo Economicus* Could Choose His Own Utility Function, Would He Want One with a Conscience?" *American Economic Review* 77:593–604.

Frank, Robert. 1988. *Passions Within Reason: The Strategic Role of the Emotions.* New York: Norton.

Frank, Robert. 1997a. *Microeconomics and Behavior.* New York: McGraw-Hill.

Frank, Robert. 1997b. "The Frame of Reference as a Public Good." *Economic Journal* 107:1832–47.

Frankfurt, Harry. 1971. "Freedom of the Will and the Concept of the Person." *Journal of Philosophy* 68:5–20.

Frey, Bruno. 1997a. *Not Just for the Money: An Economic Theory of Personal Motivation.* Northampton: Edward Elgar.

Frey, Bruno. 1997b. "On the Relationship between Intrinsic and Extrinsic Work Motivation." *International Journal of Industrial Organization* 15:427–39.

Frey, Bruno, and I. Bohnet. 1995. "Institutions Affect Fairness: Experimental Investigations." *Journal of Institutional and Theoretical Economics* 151:286–303.

Frey, Bruno, and R. Jegen. 2001. "Motivation Crowding Theory." *Journal of Economic Surveys* 15:589–623.

Friedman, Milton. 1953. *Essays in Positive Economics.* Chicago: University of Chicago Press.

Galbraith, John K. 1958. *The Affluent Society.* New York: New American Library.

George, David. 2001. *Preference Pollution.* Ann Arbor: University of Michigan Press.

Gewirth, Alan. 1978. *Reason and Morality.* Chicago: University of Chicago Press.

Gewirth, Alan. 1992. "Human Dignity as the Basis of Rights." In *The Constitution of Rights,* ed. M. Meyer and W. Parent. Ithaca: Cornell University Press.

Gewirth, Alan. 1996. *The Community of Rights.* Chicago: University of Chicago Press.

Gibbons, R. 1992. *Game Theory for Applied Economics.* Princeton: Princeton University Press.

Gilbert, Margaret. 1989. *On Social Facts.* Princeton: Princeton University Press.

Gilligan, Carol. 1982. *In a Different Voice: Psychological Theory and Women's Development.* Cambridge: Harvard University Press.

Gneezy, Uri. 2005. "Deception: The Role of Consequences." *American Economic Review* 95:384–94.

Greene, Aleza. 1999. "Honesty in Organizations: Perceptions of the Corporate Environment and Their Impact on Individual Behavior." PhD diss., Department of Psychology, Brandeis University.

Grossman, Samuel, and Oliver Hart. 1986. "The Costs and Benefits of Ownership: A Theory of Vertical and Lateral Integration." *Journal of Political Economy* 94: 691–719.

Grotius, Hugo. 1949. *The Law of War and Peace.* Translated by Louise Loomis. Roslyn, NY: Walter J. Black.

Halfon, Marl. 1989. *Integrity: A Philosophical Inquiry.* Philadelphia: Temple University Press.

Harcourt, Edward. 1998. "Integrity, Practical Deliberation, and Utilitarianism." *Philosophical Quarterly* 48:189–98.

Hargreaves Heap, S., and Y. Varoufakis. 1995. *Game Theory: A Critical Introduction.* London: Routledge.

Hart, Oliver, and Bengt Holmstrom. 1987. "The Theory of Contracts." In *Advances in Economic Theory: Fifth World Congress,* ed. T. Bewley. Cambridge: Cambridge University Press.

Hausman, David, and Michael McPherson. 2006. *Economic Analysis and Moral Philosophy.* 2nd ed. Cambridge: Cambridge University Press.

Hayek, Friedrich. 1945. "The Use of Knowledge in Society." *American Economic Review* 35:519–30.

Heath, Chip. 1999. "On the Social Psychology of Agency Relationships: Lay Theories of Motivation Overemphasize Extrinsic Incentives." *Organizational Behavior and Human Decision Processes* 78:25–62.

Held, Virginia. 1990. "Mothering versus Contract." In *Beyond Self-Interest,* ed. J. Mansbridge. Chicago: University of Chicago Press.

Hertel, Shareen, and Lanse Minkler. 2007. "Economic Rights: The Terrain." In *Economic Rights: Conceptual, Measurement, and Policy Issues,* ed. S. Hertel and L. Minkler, 1–35. Cambridge: Cambridge University Press.

Hodgson, Geoffrey. 2004. "Opportunism Is Not the Only Reason Why Firms Exist: Why an Explanatory Emphasis on Opportunism May Mislead Management Strategy." *Industrial and Corporate Change* 13:401–18.

Hoffman, M. 1991. "Empathy, Social Cognition, and Moral Action." In *Handbook of Moral Behavior and Development,* ed. W. Kurtines and J. Gerwitz, vol. 1, *Theory.* Hillsdale, NJ: Lawrence Erlbaum.

Hollis, Martin, and Robert Sugden. 1993. "Rationality in Action." *Mind* 102:1–35.

Holmes, Stephen. 1990. "The Secret History of Self-Interest." In *Beyond Self-Interest,* ed. J. Mansbridge. Chicago: University of Chicago Press.

Holmstrom, Bengt. 1982. "Moral Hazard in Teams." *Bell Journal of Economics* 13:324–40.

Honderich, Ted, ed. 1995. *The Oxford Companion to Philosophy.* Oxford: Oxford University Press.

Iannaccone, Laurence R. 1998. "Introduction to the Economics of Religion." *Journal of Economic Literature* 36:1465–96.

Ichniowski, Casey, and Kathryn Shaw. 2003. "Beyond Incentive Pay: Insiders' Estimates of the Value of Complementary Human Resource Management Practices." *Journal of Economic Perspectives* 17:155–80.

Isaac, R. Mark, and James M. Walker. 1988. "Costly Communication: An Experiment in a Nested Public Goods Problem." In *Laboratory Research in Political Economy,* ed. T. Palfrey. Ann Arbor: University of Michigan Press.

Jehle, Geoffrey, and Philip Reny. 1998. *Advanced Microeconomic Theory.* Reading, MA: Addison-Wesley.

Jencks, Christopher. 1990. "Varieties of Altruism." In *Beyond Self-Interest,* ed. J. Mansbridge. Chicago: University of Chicago Press.

Jensen, Michael, and William Meckling. 1976. "Theory of the Firm: Managerial Behavior, Agency Costs, and Capital Structure." *Journal of Financial Economics* 3:305–60.

Jonson, Ben. 2003. *Volpone.* Ed. R. Watson. 2d ed. London: A & C Black.

Kahneman, Daniel. 2003. "A Psychological Perspective on Economics." *American Economic Review* 93:162–68.

Kahneman, Daniel, Jack Knetsch, and Richard Thaler. 1986. "Fairness as a Constraint on Profit Seeking." *American Economic Review* 76:728–41.

Kalt, Joseph, and Mark Zupan. 1984. "Capture and Ideology in the Economic Theory of Politics." *American Economic Review* 74:279–300.

Kandel, Eugene, and Edward Lazear. 1992. "Peer Pressure and Partnerships." *Journal of Political Economy* 100:801–17.

Kant, Immanuel. 1785. *Grounding for the Metaphysics of Morals; with On a Supposed Right to Lie because of Philanthropic Concerns.* Translated by J. Ellington. Indianapolis: Hackett, 1993.

Keohane, Robert. 1990. "Empathy and International Regimes." In *Beyond Self-Interest,* ed. J. Mansbridge. Chicago: University of Chicago Press.

Klein, Benjamin, R. Crawford, and Armen Alchian. 1978. "Vertical Integration, Appropriable Rents, and the Competitive Contracting Process." *Journal of Law and Economics* 21:297–326.

Klein, Benjamin, and Keith Leffler. 1980. "The Role of Market Forces in Assuring Contractual Performance." *Journal of Political Economy.*

Kogut, Bruce, and Udo Zander. 1992. "Knowledge of the Firm, Combinative Capabilities, and the Replication of Technology." *Organization Science* 3:383–97.

Kogut, Bruce, and Udo Zander. 1996. "What Firms Do? Coordination, Identity, and Learning." *Organization Science* 7 (5): 502–18.

Kohlberg, Lawrence. 1984. *Essays on Moral Development.* Vol. 2, *The Psychology of Moral Development.* San Francisco: Harper and Row.

Konow, James. 1996. "A Positive Theory of Fairness." *Journal of Economic Behavior and Organization* 31:13–35.

Korsgaard, Christine. 1986. "Skepticism about Practical Reason." *Journal of Philosophy* 83:5–26. Reprinted in *Moral Discourse and Practice: Some Philosophical Approaches,* S. Darwall, A. Gibbard, and P. Railton. New York: Oxford University Press, 1997.

Korsgaard, Christine. 1994. "The Sources of Normativity." In *The Tanner Lectures on Human Values,* vol. 15, ed. G. Peterson. Salt Lake City: University of Utah Press. Reprinted in *Moral Discourse and Practice: Some Philosophical Approaches,* S. Darwall, A. Gibbard, and P. Railton. New York: Oxford University Press, 1997.

Kuran, Timur. 1990. "Private and Public Preferences." *Economics and Philosophy* 6:1–26.

Kuran, Timur. 1995. *Private Truths, Public Lies.* Cambridge: Harvard University Press.

Kuran, Timur. 1998. "Moral Overload and Its Alleviation." In *Economics, Values, and Organization,* ed. A. Ben-Ner and L. Putterman. Cambridge: Cambridge University Press.

Landy, F. J., and W. S. Becker. 1987. "Motivation Theory Reconsidered." *Research in Organizational Behavior* 9:1–38.

Langlois, Richard. 1992. "Transaction Costs in Real Time." *Industrial and Corporate Change* 1:99–127.

Lao-tzu. 1988. *Tao Te Ching*. Trans. S. Mitchell. New York: HarperCollins.
Lauren, Paul G. 1998. *The Evolution of International Human Rights*. Philadelphia: University of Pennsylvania Press.
Lawson, Tony. 1997. *Economics and Reality*. New York: Routledge.
Lazonick, William. 1990. *Competitive Advantage on the Shop Floor*. Cambridge: Harvard University Press.
Ledyard, John. 1995. "Public Goods: A Survey of Experimental Research." In *Handbook of Experimental Economics*, ed. J. Kagel and A. Roth. Princeton: Princeton University Press.
Levine, David. 1991. "You Get What You Pay For: Tests of Efficiency Wage Theories in the United States and Japan." Working paper, University of California, Berkeley. http://repositories.cdlib.org/iir/iiwps/iirwps-026–91.
Little, Brian. 1983. "Personal Projects: A Rationale and Method for Investigation." *Environment and Behavior* 15:273–309.
Loasby, Brian. 1998. "The Organization of Capabilities." *Journal of Economic Behavior and Organization* 35:139–60.
Lobban, Richard. 1994. "Pigs and Their Prohibition." *International Journal of Middle Eastern Studies* 26:57–75.
Longley, Neil. 2003. "Modeling the Legislator as an Agent for the Party: The Effects of Strict Party Discipline on Legislator Voting Behavior." *Contemporary Economic Policy* 21:490–99.
Lutz, Mark. 1993. "The Utility of Multiple Utility: A Comment on Brennan." *Economics and Philosophy* 9:145–54.
MacLeod, Bently, and D. Parent. 1999. "Job Characteristics and the Form of Compensation." *Research in Labor Economics* 18:177–242.
Mailath, George. 1998. "Do People Play Nash Equilibrium? Lessons from Evolutionary Game Theory." *Journal of Economic Literature* 36:1347–74.
Maki, Uskali. 1988. "How to Combine Rhetoric and Realism in the Methodology of Economics." *Economics and Philosophy* 4:89–109.
Mansbridge, Jane. 1990. *Beyond Self-Interest*. Chicago: University of Chicago Press.
Mansbridge, Jane. 1998. "Starting with Nothing: On the Impossibility of Grounding Norms Solely in Self-Interest." In *Economics, Values, and Organization*, ed. A. Ben-Ner and L. Putterman. Cambridge: Cambridge University Press.
Margolis, Howard. 1982. *Selfishness, Altruism, and Rationality*. Cambridge: Cambridge University Press.
Marwell, G., and R. Ames. 1981. "Economists Free Ride. Does Anyone Else?" *Journal of Public Economics* 15:295–310.
McFall, Lynne. 1987. "Integrity." *Ethics* 98:5–20.
McGraw, Kathleen. 1998. "Manipulating Public Opinion with Moral Justification." *Annals of the American Academy of Political Science* 560:129–42.
McGregor, Ian, and Brian Little. 1998. "Personal Projects, Happiness, and Meaning: On Doing Well and Being Yourself." *Journal of Personality and Social Psychology* 74:494–512.
Miceli, Thomas. 1997. *Economics of the Law: Torts, Contracts, Property, Litigation*. Oxford: Oxford University Press.
Minkler, Alanson. 1993a. "The Problem with Dispersed Knowledge: Firms in Theory and Practice." *KYKLOS* 46:569–87.

Minkler, Alanson. 1993b. "Knowledge and Internal Organization." *Journal of Economic Behavior and Organization* 21:17–30.

Minkler, Lanse. 1999. "The Problem with Utility: Toward a Non-Consequentialist/Utility Theory Synthesis." *Review of Social Economy* 67:4–24.

Minkler, Lanse. 2003. "Managing Moral Motivations." Working paper, Department of Economics, University of Connecticut, www.repec.org.

Minkler, Lanse. 2004. "Shirking and Motivations in Firms: Survey Evidence on Attitudes." *International Journal of Industrial Organization* 22:863–84.

Minkler, Lanse, and Thomas Miceli. 2004. "Lying, Integrity, and Cooperation." *Review of Social Economy* 62:27–50.

Nagel, Thomas. 1978. *The Possibility of Altruism.* Princeton: Princeton University Press. Excerpts reprinted in *Moral Discourse and Practice: Some Philosophical Approaches,* ed. S. Darwall, A. Gibbard, and P. Railton. New York: Oxford University Press, 1997.

Nagin, Daniel, James Rebitzer, Seth Sanders, and Lowell Taylor. 2002. "Monitoring, Motivation, and Management: The Determinants of Opportunistic Behavior in a Field Experiment." *American Economic Review* 92 (4): 850–73.

Nelson, Julie. 1999. "Of Markets and Martyrs: Is It OK to Pay Well for Care?" *Feminist Economics* 5:43–59.

Nelson, Richard, and Sydney Winter. 1982. *An Evolutionary Theory of Change.* Cambridge: Harvard University Press.

North, Douglass. 1990. *Institutions, Institutional Change, and Economic Performance,* Cambridge: Cambridge University Press.

O'Driscoll, Gerald, and Mario Rizzo. 1985. *The Economics of Time and Ignorance.* New York: Basil Blackwell.

Opotow, Susan. 1990. "Moral Exclusion and Injustice: An Introduction." *Journal of Social Issues* 46:1–20.

Osterloh, Margit, Jetta Frost, and Bruno Frey. 2002. "The Dynamics of Motivation on New Organizational Forms." *International Journal of the Economics of Business* 9 (1): 61–77.

Oswald, Andrew. 1997. "Happiness and Economic Performance." *Economic Journal* 107:1815–31.

Page, Roger, and James Bode. 1982. "Inducing Changes in Moral Reasoning." *Journal of Psychology* 112:113–19.

Pogge, Thomas. 2002. *World Poverty and Human Rights: Cosmopolitan Responsibilities and Reforms.* Cambridge: Polity Press.

Poole, Keith, and Howard Rosenthal. 1996. "Are Legislators Ideologues or the Agents of Constituents?" *European Economic Review* 40:707–17.

Prahalad, C. K., and G. Hamel. 1990. "The Core Competence of the Corporation." *Harvard Business Review* 68:79–91.

Prendergast, Canice. 1999. "The Provision of Incentives in Firms." *Journal of Economic Literature* 37:7–63.

Puka, B. 1991. "Toward a Redevelopment of Kohlberg's Theory: Preserving Essential Structure, Removing Controversial Content." In *Handbook of Moral Behavior and Development,* ed. W. Kurtines and J. Gerwitz, vol. 1, *Theory.* Hillsdale, NJ: Lawrence Erlbaum.

Quirk, Paul. 1990. "Deregulation and the Politics of Ideas in Congress." In *Beyond Self-Interest,* ed. J. Mansbridge. Chicago: University of Chicago Press.

Rabin, Mathew. 1993. "Incorporating Fairness into Game Theory and Economics." *American Economic Review* 83:1281–1302.
Rawls, John. 1971. *A Theory of Justice.* Cambridge: Harvard University Press.
Rest, James R. 1986. *Moral Development: Advances in Research and Theory.* New York: Praeger.
Rest, James R., and S. Thoma. 1986. "Educational Programs and Interventions." In *Moral Development: Advances in Research and Theory,* ed. J. R. Rest. New York: Praeger.
Robertson, John, and Michael Stocker. 1992. "Externalism and Internalism." In *Encyclopedia of Ethics,* ed. L. Becker and C. Becker. New York: Garland.
Ross, William D. 1939. *Foundation of Ethics.* London: Oxford University Press.
Rousseau, Denise. 1995. *Psychological Contracts in Organizations.* Thousand Oaks, CA: Sage.
Rousseau, Denise, and Judi Parks. 1993. "The Contracts of Individuals and Organizations." *Research in Organizational Behavior* 15:1–43.
Sally, David. 1995. "Conversation and Cooperation in Social Dilemmas: A Meta-Analysis of Experiments from 1958–1992." *Rationality and Society* 7:58–92.
Samuelson, Larry. 2002. "Evolution and Game Theory." *Journal of Economic Perspectives* 16:47–66.
Sappington, David. 1991. "Incentives in Principal-Agent Relationships." *Journal of Economic Perspectives* 5:45–66.
Schneider, Friedrich, and Werner Pommerehne. 1981. "Free-Riding and Collective Action: An Experiment in Public Microeconomics." *Quarterly Journal of Economics* 96:689–704.
Searle, J. R. 2001. *Rationality in Action,* Cambridge: MIT Press.
Self, Donnie, Fredric Wolinsky, and DeWitt Baldwin. 1989. "The Effect of Teaching Medical Ethics on Medical Students' Moral Reasoning." *Academic Medicine,* 64:755–59.
Sen, Amartya. 1978. "Rational Fools: A Critique of the Behavioral Foundations of Economic Theory." In *Scientific Models and Men,* ed. H. Haris. London: Oxford University Press.
Sen, Amartya. 1985. "Goals, Commitment, and Identity." *Journal of Law, Economics, and Organization* 1:341–55.
Sen, Amartya. 1998. "Foreword." In *Economics, Values, and Organization,* ed. A. Ben-Ner and L. Putterman. Cambridge: Cambridge University Press.
Sen, Amartya. 2001. *Development as Freedom.* New York: Knopf.
Sen, Amartya, and Bernard Williams, eds. 1982. *Utilitarianism and Beyond.* Cambridge: Cambridge University Press.
Sennett, Richard. 1998. *The Corrosion of Character.* New York: Norton.
Sethi, Rajiv, and E. Somanathan. 2003. "Understanding Reciprocity." *Journal of Economic Behavior and Organization* 50:1–23.
Seul, Jeffrey. 1999. "Ours Is the Way of God: Religion, Identity, and Intergroup Conflict." *Journal of Peace Research* 36:553–69.
Shanteau, J., and P. Harrison. 1991. "The Perceived Strength of an Implied Contract: Can It Withstand Financial Temptation?" *Organizational Behavior and Human Decision Processes* 49:1–21.
Shapiro, Carl. 1983. "Premiums for High Quality Products as Returns to Reputations." *Quarterly Journal of Economics* 98:659–80.

Shapiro, Carl, and Joseph Stiglitz. 1984. "Equilibrium Unemployment as a Worker Discipline Device." *American Economic Review* 74:433–44.

Shavell, Steven. 2003. "Economic Analysis of Contract Law." NBER Working Paper no. 9696, http:/www.nber.org.papers/w9696.

Shue, Henry. 1980. *Basic Rights: Subsistence, Affluence, and U.S. Foreign Policy.* Princeton: Princeton University Press.

Shue, Henry. 1988. "Mediating Duties." *Ethics* 98:687–704.

Smart, John, and Bernard Williams. 1973. *Utilitarianism: For and Against.* London: Cambridge University Press.

Smith, John M. 1982. *Evolution and the Theory of Games.* Cambridge: Cambridge University Press.

Smith, J. M., and G. Price. 1972. "The Logic of Animal Conflict." *Nature* 246:15–18.

Snarey, John. 1985. "Cross-Cultural Universality of Social-Moral Development: A Critical Review of Kohlbergian Research." *Psychological Bulletin* 97:202–32.

Sosis, Richard, and Candace Alcorta. 2003. "Signaling, Solidarity, and the Sacred: The Evolution of Religious Behavior." *Evolutionary Anthropology* 12:264–74.

Sugden, Robert. 1986. *The Economics of Rights, Cooperation, and Welfare.* Oxford: Blackwell.

Sugden, Robert. 2001. "Ken Binmore's Evolutionary Social Theory." *Economic Journal* 111:F213–F243.

Sunstein, Cass. 2004. *The Second Bill of Rights.* New York: Basic Books.

Taylor, Gabriele. 1971. "Integrity." *Proceedings of the Aristotelian Society Supplement* 55:143–59.

Teece, David. 1980. "Economics of Scope and Scope of an Enterprise." *Journal of Economic Behavior and Organization* 1:223–47.

Teece, David. 1982. "Towards an Economic Theory of the Multiproduct Firm." *Journal of Economic Behavior and Organization* 3:39–63.

Tenbrunsel, Ann. 1998. "Misrepresentation and Expectations of Misrepresentation in an Ethical Dilemma: The Role of Incentives and Temptation." *Academy of Management Journal* 41:330–39.

Tooby, John, and Leda Cosmides. 1989. "Evolutionary Psychologists Need to Distinguish Between the Evolutionary Process, Ancestral Selection Pressures, and Psychological Mechanisms." *Behavioral and Brain Sciences* 4:724–25.

Tourangeau, Roger, L. J. Lips, and Kenneth Rasinski. 2000. *The Psychology of Survey Response.* Cambridge: Cambridge University Press.

Trevino, Linda. 1992. "Moral Reasoning and Business Ethics: Implications for Research, Education, and Management." *Journal of Business Ethics* 11:445–59.

Tronto, Jane. 1993. *Moral Boundaries: A Political Argument for an Ethic of Care.* London: Routledge.

Turner, Nick, Julian Barling, Olga Epitropaki, Vicki Butcher, and Caroline Milner. 2002. "Transformational Leadership and Moral Reasoning." *Journal of Applied Psychology* 87:304–11.

van Staveren, Irene. 2001. *The Values of Economics: An Aristotelian Perspective.* London: Routledge.

Walker, Lawrence. 1984. "Sex Differences in the Development of Moral Reasoning: A Critical Review." *Child Development* 55:677–91.

Walker, Lawrence. 1991. "Sex Differences in Moral Reasoning." In *Handbook of Moral*

Behavior and Development, ed. W. Kurtines and J. Gerwitz, vol. 2, *Research.* Hillsdale, NJ: Lawrence Erlbaum.

Welch, Patrick J., and J. J. Mueller. 2001. "The Relationships of Religion to Economics." *Review of Social Economy* 59:185–202.

White, Mark. 2006. "Multiple Utilities and Weakness of Will: A Kantian Perspective." *Review of Social Economy* 64(1): 1–20.

Williamson, Oliver. 1975. *Markets and Hierarchies: Analysis and Antitrust Implications.* New York: Free Press.

Williamson, Oliver. 1985. *The Economic Institutions of Capitalism.* New York: Free Press.

Williamson, Oliver. 1996. "Economic Organization: The Case for Candor." *Academy of Management Review* 21:49–57.

Wren, Thomas. 1991. *Caring About Morality.* Cambridge: MIT Press.

Index